The SmallIvy Book of Investing

Book 1: Investing to Grow Wealthy

by Joseph Sheeley, Ph.D.

Edited by Tanya Sheeley and Joseph Sheeley

The SmallIvy Book of Investing
Book 1: Investing to Grow Wealthy

ISBN:978-1-490-32550-7

This edition first printing, March 2014.

Dedication

This book is dedicated to my father, William F. Sheeley, who passed down his interest and investing skills to me.

Foreword

This book presents more than investing tips and tricks. It provides a life plan for those who wish to become wealthy. The difference between those on a middle class income who remain in the middle class, or who even become very poor in old age, and those who become wealthy is based on three factors:

1) Debt, 2) Spending, and 3) Investing.

1) **Debt:** Debt causes people to spend far more for things than they would if they waited and paid cash. Indeed, probably half of most people's income goes towards paying interest on debt over their lifetimes.
2) **Spending:** Even for those who don't go into debt, those who spend every dollar they make cannot take advantage of the wealth multiplication effects of investing, which are truly amazing.
3) **Investing:** Finally, investing allows individuals to earn money once through work and then multiply it many times over through capital gains and interest. One can work and save up quite a bit by putting money into a bank account, but one could also dig a canal using a shovel if given enough time and determination. Investing is like using a backhoe instead.

The book is obviously an outgrowth of my blog, *The Small Investor* (www.smallivy.wordpress.com), but all of the writings have been carefully integrated to create a coherent book. I've tried to read a book that was the result of a series of blog posts being simply assembled into a book. I would never subject anyone else to that.

Without further ado, let's get started.

Introduction

Many people dabble in the stock market. Just like the gambler in Las Vegas, people spend their time tracking different stocks, buying and selling on the latest news, and generally not making much money at the end of the day. The 1990's saw the rise of the penny ante day trader. These individuals would sit at home on their computers or go to rooms full of workstations where they would attempt to make money trading stocks as they went up or down by quarters or eighths of a dollar.

They had visions of trading during the mornings and then playing golf in the afternoons. It was shown that an individual would need to be right about 80% of the time to make a profit this way, after paying all the fees and commissions. Obviously very few people did well over time.

For some who have already made their fortune through running a business or other means, the stock market is merely a form of entertainment – a way to get a little excitement during otherwise bland days. These people are not investors and they will never really make much from their activities. It just gives them battle stories to tell at parties.

A true investor is like the fisherman on the American frontier back in the 1800's. Unlike the modern angler who plays around with different lures and may throw back much of his catch, the frontiersman needed to catch fish to eat. He would do what was effective, like placing a net under a waterfall or building a fish trap, rather than what was sporting. He did what worked, even if it wasn't particularly exciting.

Investing for growing wealth, what I refer to as *serious investing*, is not exciting. It is not the talk of cocktail parties and chit chat for the water cooler. It is doing what works and doing whatever is needed to put the odds in one's favor.

A serious investor is not the favorite of the broker since he rarely trades. He builds up large positions in a few great companies and then holds for years or even decades. He buys companies, not stocks. The price patterns of stocks, *e.g.* trends, ceilings, floors, etc... are not important to him except perhaps as a way to get a better price on a purchase or a sale.

The serious investor saves and invests a portion of his income because he understands that it is worth the delay of gratification to have a steady stream of revenue that requires no additional labor. He understands compound interest and knows that to become wealthy, one must *receive* interest instead of *pay* interest each month. The serious investor first wants to use investing to grow wealth and thereby gain economic freedom. Once there, he then wants to be able to ensure a lifelong stream of income without losing the principle he worked so hard to build.

This book is for the small investor who is serious about growing and then maintaining wealth. It first presents a strategy for a young investor with a long time to invest (30-50 years) who has little money and wants to grow assets. This strategy is not the typical investment spiel about diversification, proper balances of stocks and bonds, etc... provided by many financial advisers. It is not that diversification is a bad thing, it is that diversification is designed to preserve capital, not grow capital. The goal of this book is to present strategies to beat the market, not just match it, at least while one is young and has little capital to protect.

The strategy presented for the new investor is to invest concentrated amounts in a few stocks that one believes are going to grow for years and years, and then hold them for years and years. One wants to catch the next Microsoft, IBM, or Cisco. One may get a few losers along the way, but one big winner will make up for a lot of losers. As gains are made, some of the money is diversified into mutual funds and spread among a greater number of stocks to preserve the gains.

The book then presents strategies for the investor later in life who has grown a substantial portfolio and would like to preserve it while gaining some income for living expenses. It is here that diversification is increased and cash is maintained to reduce the risk of market fluctuations affecting one's income stream. Some exposure to equities is maintained even at this stage, however, as a hedge against inflation, but mutual funds are more important.

Information on stock picking is not included in this book, but will be included in a second book. Indeed, stock picking is worthy of its own book since there is a lot of information one must absorb before becoming a good stock picker. Even then it is a craft that is learned through experience rather than something that could be distilled down into a procedure.

Having dispensed with the preliminaries, let's end this introduction with a brief summary of the reasons for wanting to become wealthy. It goes well beyond the superficial lifestyle portrayed by celebrities and rock stars. In fact, if the reader is looking to have lavish parties and buy tons of superficial things, he will be sadly disappointed. The lifestyle of celebrities is more due to their large incomes than their money management skills. People who attain and hold onto wealth have nice things but tend to be more frugal than the average NFL quarterback.

Instead, the reason for becoming wealthy is to have freedom and security. The ability to just pay for things when life's little disasters happen. To have all the things that coworkers have, but to actually own them rather than rent them with a credit card and a home equity loan. To not always be living on the edge of default if a paycheck is lost. To be able to choose a job you love, instead of working to support a lifestyle.

It is also ethical to live in an economically sustainable fashion. Indeed, there is virtue in the growth and maintenance of wealth and many benefits to society. In the very least, those who can take care of themselves don't burden others. It is also those who are firmly on the shore who can best rescue others who are drowning. It is the people who have money who are able to support churches, charities, and neighbors.

Chapter 1
Reasons for Investing

Economic freedom or *financial independence* is the state where earning an income is no longer a concern since one has the resources to support oneself and one's family indefinitely. Economic freedom gives one the ability to choose a profession out of interest rather than out of necessity. One does not need to work to put food on the table or pay the rent. One works because one chooses to do so and gets a greater reward than money from doing it.

Investing is an important step in the ultimate goal of gaining and maintaining economic freedom. While some individuals make a good income and are able to buy a lot of luxuries, many of these people are still living paycheck-to-paycheck since they spend money as fast as they make it. Any interruption in their income would cause them great financial hardship. Most people see millions of dollars flow through their hands during their working lifetimes and yet end up with little to show for it when they retire.

Despite what you may hear about the decline of the middle class, the majority of people who are millionaires today are first generation wealthy. This means they did not come from wealthy households, but instead made their way up from the middle and lower classes. The way that many millionaires become and stay wealthy is by using their income for acquiring assets, such as stocks, bonds, and real estate and then using income generated by those assets to both pay for expenses and acquire more assets.

Rather than spending all of the money that they earn directly, they put it to work, providing an additional income to supplement their pay. They have their cake and eat it too. Rather than taking out a loan when the air conditioner needs

1

fixing, they have the cash available since they have extra money coming in from stocks and rental houses. They also spend a lot less of their money paying interest, which makes it even easier to pay cash for things.

In trying to save and build wealth, obviously the greater your income, the easier it is. As I like to say, the bigger your shovel the easier it is to move dirt. Some people have a big shovel because of a good paying job or a talent that they can sell. Running a business can also provide a big shovel since your income potential is effectively limitless. Many people aren't cut out to run a business though and prefer the ease and (at least apparent) security of a paycheck. For those people, investing provides a way to be a partial owner in a business without the paperwork.

While one can become wealthy through work and diligent saving, investing makes it far easier, particularly for those without a high income job, because one does not need to earn all of the money oneself. By letting others use your money and pay you a percentage of the profits, you receive money without putting out extra labor. Each new asset acquired – each share of stock, each bond, each rental property – adds to your income stream. One can create an income stream that grows into an upper-class income with time even if starting with only a middle-class income. Eventually one will make more from these assets than one does from working.

When wealthy individuals – or those who will become wealthy – spend their money on things, they tend to put more money into things that go up in value and less in things that go down. Cars go down in value, so they would tend to buy a less expensive but adequate car. They would also buy one that is 2-4 years old to save on the depreciation. Fine furniture goes up in value, so they might spend more on a nice dresser or table, perhaps buying from an estate sale or antique shop rather than a retail furniture store. A home can be a good investment, but they would not buy a McMansion in a new trendy neighborhood because it would be difficult to predict the future price. They instead would buy an older, well-constructed house in an established neighborhood that has had a history of appreciation.

Note that above I talked about assets but have not really provided a definition. An asset is something that provides income to the owner, while a liability is something that requires money from the owner. If one acquires an asset, one's income will increase. For example, if one buys $1,000 worth of a stock paying a 5% dividend, one will have increased one's income by $50 per year, not including and price changes in the stock. If it is stock in a stable company like Clorox or Proctor and Gamble, one could also expect to sell the shares at a future date for at least the amount paid, so the purchase of the shares does not result in a destruction of the money used for their purchase. The shares of stock are just a form of storage in an inflationary environment. Just as with the piece of fine furniture, the money could be retrieved at a later date if desired.

One becomes financially independent when one has enough assets to meet one's income needs, which are dictated by one's liabilities. Obviously this can be achieved by increasing assets or decreasing liabilities. Becoming financially independent generally involves a combination of the two. Furthermore, if one can spend less than one makes, such that the extra income from assets can be used to acquire more assets, one can grow one's income exponentially.

Investments, in particular common stocks, are an important form of assets to hold. Unlike furniture and fine artwork, common stocks are easy to buy and sell and require little maintenance, other than tracking income and gains for taxes.

3

Also, in buying shares in a company, one is able to harness the skills and labor of various brilliant entrepreneurs and managers for one's own gain. When one buys shares of Berkshire Hathaway, one can take advantage of Warren Buffett's investing skills. Buy shares of Coca Cola and one now has an entire team of talented managers working to provide profits. It is a way to gain some of the wealth building power of starting a business without the hassle and risks of starting a business (with, of course, less control and profit potential than that which would come from actually starting a business).

By accumulating assets over a career, one is able to generate more and more income, eventually reaching the goal of financial independence. This is not a glamorous, get-rich-quick scheme that appears on late night television. One won't be sitting by a pool while checks magically appear in the mailbox within the first month as shown in the infomercials. It will take many years. But then again, if those schemes advertised on late-night television really worked, why would they be selling seminars since they could generate all the income they wanted?

Financial independence is out there for anyone who is willing to delay spending, buy assets, and then use a portion of the income generated by the assets to buy things rather than spending income from labor. Do the work once and then receive the benefits over your lifetime.

The Roles of Assets

Assets play an important role both in the accumulation of wealth through their growth in value and the preservation of wealth through the generation of income. Once one becomes wealthy one can spend money generated by the assets and never actually touch the money that was saved; therefore, one could go on indefinitely without another income stream.

4

There are therefore two main reasons for investing and different types of assets that are used for each reason. The first reason is to gain wealth in the first place. During this time one generally has another source of income and therefore can allow profits to compound and assets to grow. The second is to gain income for current expenses while preserving wealth. The type of securities selected and the amount of diversification utilized when assets are used for each of these two objectives are different.

Professional money managers often talk about a percentage of stocks and bonds that individuals should hold. This percentage is based on one's time frame and tolerance for risk. The old rule of thumb was to hold the percentage of bonds in your account equal to your age. A twenty year old would therefore hold 80% stocks and 20% bonds. A 60-year old would hold 40% stocks and 60% bonds. These figures have been revised somewhat over the years, generally by increasing the stock percentage since people are living and working longer. The percentage of stocks can also be revised downward for individuals who can't stomach the fluctuations caused by stocks.

Really this advice, however, is not entirely correct in using the terms "stocks" and "bonds." Stocks are assumed to be the risky investment while bonds are considered safe. The trouble is, some stocks (for example, utilities) fluctuate little in price and can be very predictable, while some bonds can be very risky (just ask the GM bondholders from 2008).

Really the investor should be allocating assets between high growth assets and income producing assets. The former are appropriate for growing wealth and are favored when one has a long time horizon and can tolerate more risk. The latter offer more safety and generate income for expenses but have lower returns over long periods of time. These types of investments are appropriate when one needs more security due to shorter time horizons but needs to generate current income and have some protection against inflation. The two types of assets are described further in the sections that follow.

Assets for Growing Wealth.

One can grow wealth more quickly if income is allowed to compound by reinvesting interest and dividends. Likewise, businesses will grow more quickly when they are reinvesting most or all of their profits in the business. One could have one pizza restaurant and take home the profits each night. If the business is successful, the profits may provide enough income for a family's necessities for several years (the successful restaurant, like shares of stock, is an asset).

If instead of taking home all of the profits, however, some of the money generated by the restaurant was used to expand the restaurant, add a bar or nicer tables to bring in more people, or purchase the land and building to open a second restaurant, the income generated by the restaurant would grow with time. The family would be receiving less of an income in the short-term while the expansion was ongoing, and would need to do with less or have another source of income. Later on, however, they would be doing much better because a family with ten successful restaurants would have a much greater income than one with only a single restaurant.

When a business is young and there is a lot of room to expand, the value of the business can grow quickly if most of the profits are reinvested. This is why many young companies pay little or no dividend. Because there are a lot of opportunities to expand the business, it is better for the company and the shareholders to use the cash flow for expansion and acquisition of competitors than for them to be paying profits out to shareholders.

Because of the opportunity for rapid growth and expansion, small, young companies that pay small dividends or no dividends are great for growing wealth. For example, if one invested in Amazon in the late 1990's, one would have seen the value of one's shares grow several hundred percent over the next few years. A similar investment in a bank CD would have only returned a few percent per year.

There are also tax advantages to investing in these types of businesses. If the company is paying out dividends regularly taxes are paid on those dividends, even if the money is immediately reinvested. If a company pays no dividends and the money is instead put back into the business, that money is able to compound without taxes being removed each year. The 15% or more the investor would pay in taxes is reinvested to continue to grow. The company will also save on/delay corporate income taxes if the money is reinvested to make improvements.

Growth stocks have their pitfalls, however, making them unsuitable for those with a shorter time horizon. If one were relying on an investment in Amazon in the late 1990's and selling shares periodically to generate current income, one would have been in for a nasty shock. In the early 2000s, when the internet bubble burst, the value of Amazon fell through the floor, declining in value by about 90%. One would have been lucky to even sell the shares for what one originally paid if they were bought on the way up. If bought near the top, it would be years before the loss was recouped.

For the investor who didn't need the money right away and could actually buy more shares after the fall, this would not be any great tragedy. In fact, the value of the shares has recovered and even grown a bit above their value in the late 1990s (since Amazon is now actually making a profit to justify their stock price). The income investor, however, who needed

7

the money each year and could not wait for the recovery, would have had to sell at low prices.

Another risk involves the size of the company. While young, rapidly expanding businesses can have a very high rate of return, they also more risky than larger, more established businesses. If they expand too rapidly, make a bad acquisition, or simply misread the market the effect on profits will be much more severe than it would be for larger businesses. Larger businesses can have many product lines and are in many different regions, while smaller businesses typically just have a few product lines and only a few locations. A big company like Wal-Mart can make a few missteps and recover. A small company cannot. For this reason stock in small growth companies is suitable for building wealth, but stock in large established companies is suitable for maintaining wealth.

An individual should primarily own these high growth assets when he/she is young but has another source of income – a job – for daily expenses. At this point one has little money to invest but also has a long time horizon and is not dependent on income from the assets to eat. At this stage of life it is more important to grow wealth than to preserve what one has, so the risk is justified. One can also afford to wait while a company finds its niche and expands. In other words, you don't need to pick a company that does well immediately, just one that does well sometime in the next several years. As one becomes more dependent on one's income from assets, a smaller percentage should be devoted to small growth stocks since the consequences of sharp declines becomes greater.

Stocks suitable for growing wealth have the following characteristics:

1. They tend to be young companies or companies that have undergone a radical transformation (a large new

business line or a huge restructuring in which many assets and liabilities were shed. For example, see Apple Computer).

2. They have a lot of room for expansion.
3. They are able to grow profits substantially each year.
4. They pay little or no dividend.
5. They have little or no debt. They have a lot of cash flow from current operations that allows them to grow and make acquisitions.
6. They have the ability to perform research or test new product lines using cash flow from current operations.

Examples of great growth companies in the 1980's and 1990's include Bed Bath and Beyond, Home Depot, and Starbucks. The reader is invited to review the history of these companies to get a feel for what a good growth company looks like. Note that while these were small growth companies in the past, they may not be anymore since they have largely matured.

Assets for Generating Income

As one grows older and gathers more assets, the need to protect what has been gained becomes more significant. If one has developed a portfolio of $250,000, say, over the last ten or twenty years, one would certainly not like to see it all lost in a single large position and need to start all over again. While one should still maintain some positions in fast growing companies, some of the money should be shifted into more reliable assets that are less susceptible to price declines.

As a business grows bigger, there get to be fewer and fewer good opportunities to expand. Once there is a Starbucks on every corner, adding another will just rob some of the business from those that are already there. Even if profits continue to grow rapidly, the amount of additional money that must be earned to double profits also increases. Think of how difficult it would be for Coca-Cola to double the number of sodas they sell. At that point the rate of growth of the company will slow.

Because these large companies sell a large number of products each year and have a proven business model, however, they have a reliable stream of income. There are a lot of people who make a daily trip to Starbucks on the way to work and they will not give this habit up easily. This type of company will not grow rapidly, but will also not be as likely to disappear during the next recession.

Because there are few opportunities for additional growth, it makes more sense for the company to start giving money from operations out to shareholders rather than reinvesting in the business. At this point the company is likely to start issuing a dividend each quarter. For the shareholder this means that the rate of return will be more predictable. Even if the price of the shares does not change or declines slightly, the income from the dividend will provide a return. This makes these stocks less risky. As long as the investor holds onto the shares, and the company continues to make enough money to keep paying the dividend, the investor can wait for the share price to recover before selling while collecting the dividend.

The dividend also prevents the price of the shares from dropping as rapidly since the amount of the dividend usually stays fixed, meaning that the yield paid increases as the share price drops. If the share price drops too much, the rate of return from the dividend will become so high that individuals who are investing in bonds and other assets will shift their money into the stock, thereby driving the price up. This puts an effective floor under the price of the stock.

Here again, this is only true if the company keeps making enough money to keep paying the dividend. In bad economic times, companies may cut their dividend. This is particularly true if the share price has dropped so substantially that the dividend yield is now much higher than those of the company's peers.

In addition to dividend paying stocks, there are other assets that provide stability and income. These include bonds, preferred stocks, and real estate investment trusts (REITs). There are also bank CDs and money markets, but these pay so little in interest that one will lose buying power if these are held for long periods of time. They therefore are more of a way to park money for short periods of time rather than assets.

Stocks that are suitable for retaining wealth are generally in companies that have the following characteristics:

1. They are large companies with a lot of different business lines, ideally in more than one country.
2. They are brand names (Coke, IBM, Procter and Gamble, etc...).
3. They pay a dividend that is substantial when compared to those paid by other stocks. Remember also that companies may grow their dividend over time. A stock that is paying a 2% dividend may not seem exciting, but if they are increasing their payout by 10% per year, this will double every seven years.
4. They may be in a regulated industry but have a monopoly that ensures reliable income (for example, utilities).
5. They are the largest company among their competitors.
6. They have substantial cash flow, making the dividend safe and providing substantial income for product development and operations.

An Aside – Is Growing Wealth Empty and Evil?

Aside from Gordon Gekko in *Wall Street*, with his "Greed is Good" speech, rarely do people speak well of the wealthy. Somehow someone who does well while investing and amasses a pile of money is considered evil while the guy working 9-5 and getting paid time-and-a-half for nights and weekends is good. Never mind that it is because of the investor and the entrepreneur that the 9-5 worker has a job to which to go and get paid by the hour. Even our friend, Mr. Gekko, turned out to be nothing but an evil thief in the end of the movie. The chance to paint successful capitalists as crooks is never lost in Hollywood.

There is a belief that those who make money somehow did so by taking advantage of others. The factory worker is virtuous so long as he spends every dime, the worker at the non-profit who takes in donations and distributes them is more virtuous, and the individual who advocates for the poor and the worker is saintly. The Sam Waltons, the Henry Fords, and the Andrew Carnegie's of the world are evil.

Looking at the true benefit to society, however, Henry Ford and Sam Walton had a much bigger impact and have benefited far more people than any charity worker. Thousands of people have had good jobs as car factory workers, dealership owners and employees, and car mechanics thanks to Henry Ford transforming the automobile from the plaything of the rich to the necessity of the masses. Likewise, while high earning individuals who have the time to visit several shops during the day and pay a premium for goods lament the loss of the Mom and Pop store, the fact is that Mom and Pop stores tended to just employ Mom and Pop, and maybe an odd son or daughter. Conversely, thousands find jobs at Wal-Marts across the country. Many people find first jobs at Wal-Mart, and some move into management or up the corporate ladder at other companies.

The benefit to employees, however, is less than the benefit to consumers. Think of the convenience of being able to go to the dealerships down the street and having hundreds of cars from which to choose. Likewise, thanks to Wal-Mart, people in small towns across America are able to buy all sorts of things that were once available only in big cities. And these things can be bought at any hour day or night, instead of the 10-4 hours kept by Mom and Pop. Also, the prices are far less thanks to the work of Mr. Ford and Mr. Walton than they would have been. This has led to the creation of all sorts of other businesses, many of these Mom and Pop businesses, that would not have been possible without the low-cost supplies available at Wal-Mart.

Sure, Mr. Ford and Mr. Walton did this not out of concern for their fellow man, but for profit. And sure, they both became very wealthy. The reason they became wealthy, however, was not because they cheated their customers or did something underhanded like Boss Hogg in the *Dukes of Hazzard* or Mr. Burns in *The Simpsons*.

They made very little money from each customer and most customers felt they received goods at a fair price. They became wealthy because they filled a need for millions of people. Those who make the most money in a business fulfill the most pressing needs that people have. The more pressing the need and the more people they help, the more money they make.

When investing, individuals are delaying their own pleasure–the spending of their money–in order to grow their wealth. This is not done by putting the money under a rock, but instead by supporting businesses that are providing goods and services to consumers. While it is true that most investing money doesn't go to businesses directly – stocks are traded among individuals after the stock has gone public – because there is a market for the stock, businesses are able to raise capital through initial public offerings and later through subsequent offerings, issuing bonds, and other activities. They also use stock options to compensate senior management rather than pay funds out of operations.

In investing, like in business, those who make the most money aren't the ones who are jumping in and out of various stocks or doing some complicated options trades. They are the people who put money into businesses that do the best – those that are best fulfilling the needs of their customers and society in general. So if you are a good investor and have made a lot of money, don't feel ashamed. While it always good to give and help others around you, just by investing the money you have helped a lot of people.

The second reason growing wealth is good and not evil is that you are using your gifts to take care of yourself and your family so that others do not need to do so. The first obligation of an individual is to provide for one's own needs and that of one's family. Doing so then puts one in the position to help others. It is a lot easier to help a neighbor who loses a house to a tornado if you have money in the bank instead of a stack of credit card bills.

In the bible, Jesus says it would be "easier for a camel to pass through the eye of a needle than a rich man to get into heaven." Perhaps this *is* saying that there is something evil about acquiring money. I believe, however, that Jesus meant those who are wealthy find it tempting to be distracted by their money and material things. They can start to think that they are very important because they have wealth and that they don't need God in their lives. Their downfall is that they put their wealth before God, not that the possession of wealth is fundamentally bad.

Not using the gifts given to one's best ability and to take from others when one could provide for oneself is certainly not noble either. This is shown in the parable where the three servants are given a sum of their master's money to hold. The ones who invest the money and return more than they were given are rewarded, while the one who stashed it away to preserve it was scolded. Investing is making the most of what you are given, increasing your ability to help others. Of course, I'm not going to pretend to know the judgment of God and say that just investing is enough for sainthood. It isn't a bad idea to tithe on the earnings as well.

One neat thing to do with wealth is to set up an investment specifically for giving. Maybe put $10,000 in a mutual fund and then give away 5% of the value each year. This might start out as a $500 gift, but with compounding and the addition of other funds once in a while, over time in will grow into thousands or even hundreds of thousands each year.

And don't just send a check to the first charity that sends you a letter. Have fun with it. Pay off lay away items for strangers at stores. Leave $100 tips. Maybe place a $20 under the wipers of a random car in the parking lot. Pay for the food of the next people behind you in the drive-thru. Giving can be more fun than spending if done well.

Chapter 2
Investment Options – Background

In Chapter 1 I discussed the different reasons for investing and the difference between assets designed for growing wealth and those made for maintaining wealth and providing income. A detailed description of the different types of common assets is now presented. As you have has probably already figured out, I recommend common stocks as the primary investment vehicle for a variety of reasons, but there are other options as well that can play a part during different stages of one's investing lifetime.

There are many investing options to consider and more being made each day. It is easy to get lost and confused, leading to unexpected losses. It is critical that you understand the background and risks of the various investments before committing money. In particular, an understanding what could lead to the loss of money and how much money could be lost should be had before going into an investment. As is always the case, one can never win the game if one does not know the rules.

Among the common investment/speculation choices, going from the least risky to the most risky, are:
1) savings accounts,
2) money market funds,
3) government savings bonds,
4) treasury bonds,
5) paid-for real estate,
6) municipal and corporate bonds,
7) preferred stocks,
8) common stocks,
9) penny stocks,

10) warrants, commodities, and
11) options.

Despite common stocks coming near the end of that list, meaning that they are more risky than many investment options, there are good reasons to include stocks as the primary investment in your portfolio. I will therefore begin with their description before continuing on to other asset types. I will also spend considerably more time discussing them than I will on other assets.

Common Stocks

Background
When a company needs to raise money to manufacture widgets, rent offices, and hire employees, they generally have two choices. The first option is to borrow the money by issuing bonds or going through a bank or venture capital firm. The second option is to sell off a portion of the company - and its future earnings - by issuing common stock.

When a company decides to sell shares of stock, in a process called "going public," an Initial Public Offering (IPO) is held in which a specified number of shares, representing a certain percentage of ownership in the company, is sold. The IPO is handled by one of the large security firms who is responsible for publicizing the IPO and gathering an initial group of investors.

Typically the IPO price is set by the security firm and the company based on the perceived value of the company. This value is determined by current and potential earnings. The price is then determined by dividing the perceived value by the number of shares to be offered. Once sold through the IPO, the shares are then traded among individuals based on their perception of the value of the company. If the IPO price is set too high the company will not be able to sell all of the shares or the price of the stock will drop quickly after it goes public. If set too low, the price may rocket upwards, delighting initial investors but meaning that the company could have raised far more money.

Each share of common stock represents a fractional share of the company. Each holder of common stock therefore has a say in how the company is run and gets a share of the profits. The amount of the say and the share of the profits is determined by how many shares are held. For example, in voting on propositions individuals typically get one vote per share; therefore, if an individual owns a majority of the shares, she can control the company. Likewise, dividends are issued on a per-share basis.

After the IPO, additional shares of the company may be sold, either from the percentage of control retained by the company or by further dividing the value of the company. In this latter situation, the majority of the shareholders must approve of the issuance of further shares since each share will then be worth a smaller percentage of the company after the secondary offering. Because the company receives additional funds which can be used for acquisitions, expansions, and other activities, however, the actual value of each share may not decrease (each share is worth a smaller percentage of the pie but the pie is bigger). Normally companies are able to issue additional shares without any problem since owners hold a lot of the shares, meaning they get a lot of votes, and stockholders generally go along with whatever the board proposes.

Advantages of Stocks
Common stocks are generally more risky than bonds and other investments like bank CDs since the investor is assuming an ownership stake in the company. This means that if the

company loses money, the value of the ownership, and therefore the value of each share of stock, will decrease. Despite stocks being more risky than many investment options, there are good reasons to hold them as a major portion of your portfolio. Among these:

1) Stocks can beat the rate of inflation, leading to growth in capital. Of the various investment options, stocks are one of the few that provide enough of a return to beat inflation. If you are saving for retirement decades from now, the dollars you invest today in money market funds, treasury bonds, and the like will be worth only a fraction of their value when you retire. Real estate (that you buy fully for cash) will on average just track the level of inflation (although there are special situations where you buy properties that become more desirable with time). Common and preferred stocks hold a nice place in the risk curve where you can beat inflation but still put the odds in your favor.

2) Long-term holding of stocks allows compounding through the delay of taxes. Capital gains taxes on stocks do not come due until the stock is sold. This means that investors who hold stocks for long periods of time get to enjoy the benefit of compounding for years without paying taxes on the capital gains until the shares are sold. Warren Buffett and Bill Gates have paid relatively little in the way of taxes, despite their enormous wealth, because most of their wealth is in stock in their companies. Because they sell only a few shares each year, their tax bill as a percentage of their wealth is very small.

By contrast, those earning a paycheck have 25-35% of their earnings taken by state and federal income taxes and another 13% taken by payroll taxes before they even see it. Note that if the stock is held in a mutual fund, capital gains taxes will be due if the mutual fund sells shares in the fund at a profit and distributes the gains to you even if you do not sell shares of the mutual fund. This is one reason to select funds with a low turn-over or "churn rate."

3) Investing in stocks requires much less effort than some other types of investments. Real estate can be a great investment if you know what you're doing, but you often need to have it as your hobby since it requires a lot of time outside of your normal job. If you want to buy, renovate, and resell houses, count on spending many hours at the house doing a lot of the work. Even if you contract the work out, losing much of your profit, you will rarely find someone with as much commitment to the project as you do since it is your house.

If you rent houses, count on doing a lot of repairs yourself late at night, or paying a fortune to others to do it. Because the renters are not paying the bill for repairs, it matters little to them that Sunday rates for repair men are 2 to 3 times weekday rates. They would probably be more willing to sweat a bit if they were paying for the air conditioner repairs on a Saturday night. If the landlord is paying the bill though, the extra cost matters little.

With long-term investing in stocks, you simply need to spend a little time finding stocks to purchase, call a broker or enter trades on a website, and then monitor the stocks once in a while. Because good investing is long-term and based on the business, rather than on the short-term fluctuations in price, it really doesn't require a big time commitment. Just once in a while check on things, read the annual reports to see that the company is still doing what it was when you bought it, and then leave things alone. In times when the markets are going down, taking everything with them, it is actually better to ignore your holdings for a while than to sell off in a panic at low prices.

For even less care and feeding, a set of index mutual funds can be purchased. In that case, the only maintenance required is to rebalance the money in the funds once a year. Many mutual fund companies have online tools to help with this. As retirement nears, you may spend a bit more time since funds will need to be sold to raise the cash needed for living expenses. Still, this is not more than a couple of hours per week.

While other investments deserve a place in one's portfolio, common stocks, either bought directly or through mutual funds, definitely deserve a prominent place for money that will not be needed in the next 5-10 years.

Investment Terms

Before leaving stocks and continuing onto other asset types, here is some of the common terms usually associated with stocks that should be part of any investor's vocabulary:

shares of stock- Shares of stock are fractional ownership rights in a company. Companies issue shares to gain money (called "capital") to buy equipment, make capital improvements, and generally grow their business. Once the shares are issued to the public, they are traded between individuals.

market cap- The number of shares of stock outstanding times the price per share. This gives the relative value of a company. The larger the cap, the bigger the company.

stock exchange- A stock exchange is a place where people gather to trade shares of stock. This is done by individuals who have acquired the right to do so (through the purchase of a seat on the exchange) and their employees. These "individuals" are brokerage firms, venture capital firms, and others. The brokerage firms are largely (but not always) trading shares for their clients. Most trades are now done using computers that automatically match buyers and sellers.

NYSE- The New York Stock Exchange, one of the oldest and largest exchanges. Larger stocks typically trade on the NYSE, which is also known as the "big board." Most stocks on the NYSE have three letter *ticker symbols*, although some have two or even one letter ticker symbols. (Note, ticker symbols are the symbol used to specify a stock that you now type into your computer to get a quote. When stock tickers were used, the ticker symbol and the price would be printed on a paper tape to indicate that a particular stock had traded.)

The Curb- The American Stock Exchange, a smaller exchange than the NYSE that started when a group of traders started trading outside of the NYSE on the curb of the street. The American Stock Exchange in the most common place where "exchange traded funds" trade.

NASDAQ- The National Association of Security Dealers Automated Quotation System. A newer exchange – but still decades old – made up of a network of computers. Smaller stocks tend to trade on the NASDAQ, as do many technology companies.

specialist and market maker- These are individuals involved in actually making the stock trades happen by taking the other side of the trade (for example, buying the shares from the person who would like to sell). The specialist makes money by buying the shares at the bid price and selling them at the ask price. The difference between a specialist and a market maker is an advanced topic not needed here.

bid price- The current price that someone is willing to pay for a stock.

ask price- The current price for which someone is willing to sell some shares.

the spead - This is the difference between the bid and the ask price. Typically the market maker or specialist pockets this difference by buying shares from one individual at the bid price and selling them to another individual at the ask price. Not too long ago, stocks were listed in fractions, so the spread was typically no less than 1/8, or 12.5 cents per share ($12.50 for 100 shares). More recently stocks began trading in decimals such that the smallest theoretical spread is 1 penny per share or $1 for 100 shares.

going long- Taking a position in a stock (or other equity or product) such that money is made if the price of the stock goes up. For example, buying shares of stock.

going short- The opposite of going long. Taking a position such that money will be made if the price of the stock goes down.

short sale- A trade in which an individual borrows shares of stock and sells them, thus getting the proceeds from the sale. The position is closed by later buying back the shares, hopefully at a lower price. Note that the brokerage firm normally takes care of finding the shares to borrow.

stop loss- An order to sell shares of stock if the price drops below a certain price, thereby preventing further losses.

market order- An order to buy/sell shares at whatever the current ask/bid price is when there is a seller/buyer on the other side of the trade (or a market maker willing to take the opposite side of the trade).

limit order- An order in which the stock will be bought/sold when the ask/bid is at or below/above a certain price. For example, an order to "buy 100 shares of XYZ corp at a limit of $20 or better" would be filled when the ask price was $20 per share or lower, such that the buyer would never pay more than $20 per share.

dividend- Money paid by a company to share holders who own stock on a certain date (called the "ex-dividend date"). The amount paid is based on the number of shares held (for example, 2 cents per share or $2.00 for 100 shares).

capital gain- Money made on a stock by buying shares at a lower price and selling them at a higher price.

split- An event where a company issues shares in order to reduce the price per share. For example, in a 2-for-1 split a share holder who owned 100 shares worth $20 per share would end up with 200 shares worth $10 per share. There is no net difference in the value of the holding.

Bonds

A company, a city, or another entity issues bonds when it wishes to borrow money to pay for something. A bond is a loan made to a company or another entity which typically pays a fixed interest rate for a period of time. Bonds issued by companies are called "corporate bonds," while those issued by a city are call "municipal bonds."

Most bonds are listed by the interest rate that is paid to the initial buyers of the bond, called the coupon, and an expiration date, called the maturity date. For example, if AT&T issued a bond that matures in 2020 that pays an initial rate of 9%, it would be called an AT&T 2020 9% bond. AT&T may have a whole host of bonds of different maturity dates and interest rates.

On issue a bond normally sells for $1000 per bond. The initial interest rate is set at whatever rate is expected to be needed to sell all of the bonds. Just as a consumer who has a high FICO score can often get a better rate on loans, a company that has a very good credit rating will be able to issue bonds with a lower initial interest rate, or *coupon*. Companies that have sterling credit are said to issue "investment grade" bonds, while those with poor credit are said to issue "junk bonds." The higher interest rate paid by the junk bonds makes up for the greater risk of default.

Once the bond is issued, investors can trade the bonds on the open market. It is very rare for an individual to hold a bond all of the way from first issuance to maturity. Because the bond pays a fixed amount of money each year – for example our AT&T 9% bond would pay $90 per bond each year – if the price of the bond declines the effective interest rate that the new investor receives increases. Likewise, if the bond goes up in price, the interest rate that the new investor receives will decrease. The company continues to pay the same rate, however, based on the initial loan amount since they keep paying the same amount of money per bond each year.

Because the investor holding the bond when it matures will receive the par value – normally $1000 per bond – a person who buys a bond below the par value will receive an additional amount of income if he/she holds the bond to maturity. Likewise, if one buys a bond above par value, he will get back a little less than he paid when the bond matures. The yield, taking into account this price differential, is called the "yield to maturity."

Bonds are often considered a safe investment. In fact most

investment advisers recommend keeping a certain portion of one's assets in bonds for security. There are special risks to the bond investor, however, that the investor must understand. These are covered in the next chapter.

Preferred Stocks

Preferred stock is often issued by a company for a special purpose. For example, if a company wanted to gain enough money for building a new plant, they might choose to issue preferred stock. Preferred stock might also be issued as compensation to directors or others.

The exact nature of shares of preferred stock are specified when they are issued. In general, shares of preferred stock do not represent ownership as do shares of common stock. Often holders of preferred shares do not have the right to vote in election or on other matters.

Despite the lack of ownership, preferred stocks carry many advantages to common shares. Holders of preferred shares almost always receive a higher dividend than holders of common stock. Another advantage is that holders of preferred shares often have first rights over funds of the corporation. For example, dividends of preferred shares are usually paid before those for common shares. A disadvantage of preferred stocks, however, is that the dividend for preferred shares usually is fixed when the shares are issued and does not rise as earnings increase, as will dividends on common shares.

Some preferred stocks are also *convertible*. This means that the shares can be converted into shares of common stock at some specified ratio of shares of common stock per preferred share. For example, if IBM were to issue some convertible shares, they might specify that each ten shares of preferred stock could be converted into one share of common stock.

Because of the possibility of conversion, the price of the preferred stock will tend to rise if the price of the common shares rise. In this case, the price of the preferred shares will likely never be less than 10% of the price of the common stock since 10 preferred shares can always be converted into a share of common stock.

Preferred stocks are normally suitable for wealth preservation and generation of income. Their higher yields and preferential treatment when allocating company funds tends to prevent them from falling as rapidly as shares of the common stock. In the case of convertible preferred stocks, the investor will also have the chance of receiving some appreciation since the price of the preferred shares will tend to increase – although not as rapidly – when the price of the common stock increases.

Real Estate and REITs

Many individuals invest in real estate, even if just buying a home. As the old saying goes, your home is "the biggest investment you'll ever make." Hopefully for you this will not be the case, but for many people their home is the only asset they have as they near retirement. In the past the standard practice when retiring was to sell the big family house and move into an inexpensive condo, using the proceeds from the house to pay for expenses.

Real estate investing is a bit different than simply buying a home. Income from real estate investing typically takes the form of either rental income or capital appreciation. In either case a great deal of knowledge is needed about the real estate markets and home values in the area to be able to pick the best properties and price then correctly. To quote another old saying, "All real estate is local."

Looking at the risks and returns of real estate investing, investing in paid-for real estate, where there is no mortgage, is less risky than individual stock investing and more risky than buying income securities. The return will also lag behind individual stock investing and the hassle factor is much larger. Real estate markets, however, tend to be less transparent than stock markets. This means that it is possible to find people selling real estate at well below what others are willing to pay, so an individual who is able to correctly price real estate and thereby know the difference between a great deal and a poor deal can do very well.

As many have discovered recently, buying real estate with a mortgage can be very risky. For years it was generally accepted that the price of houses always went up. Taking out a mortgage was therefore seen as safe as long as nothing happened to one's income stream such that one could no longer afford the mortgage.

Buying real estate with a mortgage, however, involves a substantial amount of what is known as *leverage*. This is the use of a little bit of money to control something much more valuable. When the value of the thing increases, one is able to make huge profits due to the large value of the thing being controlled. For example, if one buys a $500,000 house for cash and the value of the property increases by $5000, or 1%, one only makes 1%. If one puts $500 down on a $500,000 house, however, and the value of the home increases by $5,000, one will have made a 1000% profit.

During boom times, this meant that an individual could make huge profits by buying and selling houses, and there were many individuals who used the available no-money-down loans to speculate, buying several homes at a time with interest only loans. The trouble is that leverage cuts both ways. If that

$500,000 home goes down just 10% in price, suddenly one has lost $50,000 on what seemed to be a $500 investment. Couple this with a loan that one could barely afford in the first place and where the payments increase after an initial introductory period, and you have the housing crisis of 2008.

For the small investor, buying real estate with mortgages, other than one's home, is far too risky. Adding some real estate to a portfolio if it is large enough to pay cash for properties can be very useful. The advantages are that they provide a steady source of income through rents, and that the appreciation in the price of the property should at least keep pace with inflation. Again, if one buys in the right markets or finds properties that are selling at a bargain, one can even beat inflation.

The second advantage is that real estate does not tend to be correlated with the movements of other investments (2008 excepted). This means that the price and rental income received from the properties usually moves independently of the prices and returns of other assets. This adds protection to a portfolio since when your stocks are down your real estate may be up or vice-versa.

As with buying individual stocks, one will tend to do better buying individual properties, particularly if one has the knowledge to select the good properties. This requires a substantial amount of time and energy, however, since the properties must be found and all of the activities required when buying or selling a house must be performed (including paying all of those various people who have their hands out when a house changes hands). In addition, if renting one must deal with tenants who may decide to not pay the rent, trash the place, or simply call at 3 AM about the hot water heater.

For those not wanting to deal with individual properties, Real Estate Investment Trusts, or (REITs), may be the solution.

These are similar to mutual funds, in that the funds of individuals are pooled together to purchase a set of properties. The holders of the REITs then receive a share of the rent and appreciation income. Like a mutual fund, the price of the REIT will increase or decrease depending on the income being generated, the value of the properties held, and other factors. The main disadvantage is that the fees paid to the administrators of the REIT will eat into profits.

Commodities-Gold, Silver, Platinum

There are basically two types of commodities, soft commodities such as wheat, eggs, and orange juice, and hard commodities such as gold, silver, and platinum. I will not say anything further about soft commodities since these are only suitable for speculation. This is because soft commodities waste away and rot, meaning that they can only be held for a limited amount of time. Because everyone has the same information on current prices and expected supply, making money on soft commodities really comes down to luck. Speculating in soft commodities is fine if you are a multi-millionaire and want to gamble with a small portion of your fortune for fun, but it is not a way to make money.

Hard commodities are really not an investment for growing wealth either. The reason is that they do not increase in value in real terms. A pound of gold in the year 1000 will buy about the same value of merchandise, land, or labor today as it would have in 1000. Their price does fluctuate, generally increasing in value when there are tensions in the world or worry about the monetary systems, but these minor changes in price will be erased if the metals are held for long enough. They do not rot, however, so one can hold onto them indefinitely, unlike a bushel of corn where one will be forced to sell and lose money or see the value of the entire bushel vanish if corn prices fall near harvest time.

Hard commodities may have a place in a portfolio when the goal is to preserve wealth and one believes that high inflation is around the corner. As said, the buying power of materials such as gold will remain about constant over time, so they are a fairly good inflation hedge. They are certainly not perfect, however, in that it is generally necessary to pay a fee to store hard commodities and insure them or take a risk that they might be stolen if kept at home.

Stocks and real estate are also good hedges against inflation, however. The price of a company, in dollar terms, will increase if the value of the dollars are decreasing due to inflation. Likewise, the value of a piece of land will remain nearly constant if nothing about it changes. If your goal is to hide away wealth for your great, great grandchildren in a mason jar in your backyard, or you are worried about inflation and want some diversification beyond stocks and real estate, buying a small amount of gold may be worth doing. In general, however, hard commodities are dead money and investing elsewhere and saving the gold buying for jewelry is the way to go.

Derivatives – Options, Warrants LEAPs

Options
Options were originally designed to act as insurance against share declines or rapid rises. For example, if an investor owned 1000 shares of XYZ stock and was worried that it might decline in price but didn't want to sell the shares, he might buy 10 put options. The *put* options would give the investor the right, but not the obligation, to sell the shares at a predetermined price. Like any insurance contract, the contract would expire after a certain period of time. If the stock dropped below the predetermined price (called the *strike price*)

before the date the insurance contract expired, the investor would be able to sell his shares for the strike price. Like any good insurance, this limited the loss for the investor. If the price fell after the expiration date, however, the options would offer no further protection.

A similar insurance contract was created on the other side of a trade. This contract, called a *call* option, allows an investor to buy shares for a particular price before a particular date. To mirror the example given with the put option, a call option might be used by a short seller who wants protection in case the shares of a stock he has sold short rise rapidly. (In a short sale, a person sells borrowed shares and then buys them back in the market at a later date. If the price declines during that time, he makes a profit. If it rises, he takes a loss.) By owning call options on the stock he has short, his loss is limited since he can always buy back the shares at the strike price.

The most common use of options is for speculation rather than insurance. For example, a speculator may decide that Google stock is about to go up, but doesn't want to pay the $600 per share that Google is trading for that day. That investor instead could buy call options that would allow him to buy shares of Google at $600 anytime in the next three months. These options might cost $10 each. If the investor wanted to have the right to buy 1000 shares, it would cost him $10,000 :

Cost = ($10) x (100 shares/option) x (10 options).

At $600 per share, he would effectively control $600,000 worth of stock for the $10,000 speculation. If the stock then went to $650, his call options would be worth at least $50 each (because anyone who purchased them could buy the stock at $600 and immediately sell it for $650), so he would have made $40,000 on the deal. This would be a 400% profit on a stock move of less that 10%. This is what is known as leverage –

the control of a large amount of money using a little amount of money, such that small movements in the stock result in large profits.

The issue with leverage, however, is that it cuts both ways. Because the speculator needs to be right not only in the direction of the stock movement, but the timing, using options for speculation is very risky. Every minute of every day, the value of the options decays until it becomes worthless on the expiration date. If Google never moves above the strike price while the options are still in force and the options are held until expiration, the investor will lose the whole $10,000, even if Google goes to $700 the next day.

Most option contracts expire worthless, so the buying of option contracts is a losing strategy over the long-term, just like roulette. There may be reasons to use them as insurance contracts as was originally intended. There is little reason to use them otherwise unless one wants to gamble and has the resources to do so.

An exception may be the writing of covered calls, which is a strategy for making income from a stock whose price is fairly stagnant. That strategy is covered in detail in Chapter 8. Theoretically one could make returns of 15-20% writing covered calls, but my experience has been that returns are far less and it is not always worth the added hassle.

Warrants and LEAPS
Warrants are like options except they are issued by a company. Warrants generally give the holder the right to buy shares of a stock for a certain price. Like options, they expire after a certain period. The expiration time for warrants is generally several years into the future from the time they were issued. The idea is to give the buyer the opportunity to participate in the growth of the company (usually in exchange for something

else), but not dilute the value of the shares should the company not appreciate. For example, warrants might be issued to employees as incentive for trying to improve the performance of the company.

LEAPS are long-term options that are very similar to warrants except they are not issued by the company. The expiration time for LEAPS is generally one to three years. Like options, LEAPS are speculation and should not be purchased for anything other than the entertainment value. They are therefore not suitable for growing wealth.

There may be some special circumstances in which one does not wish to buy or sell a stock at the current time but would like protection in case the stock changes in price. For example, if one has a large capital gain on a stock and therefore wants to delay selling the shares until the next year to delay taxes or because tax rates are expected to fall in the future, but one is worried that the stock may decline in value before the next year. LEAPS might be suitable in such a hedging scenario. In general, however, it is usually better to just sell the stock.

Having completed a review of the basics of the common investing choices, the next chapter will discuss the relationship between risk and reward for investments. A description of the specific risks of each of the different investment choices will then be presented. Investing is all about managing risk while maximizing reward. This is done by selecting assets of appropriate volatility and diversification for one's time frame.

Chapter 3
Understanding Risk and Reward

Investing, Speculation and Trading

In dealing with assets, one may be investing, speculating, or trading. Understanding the difference is important. Investing is useful for growing wealth since it allows one to multiply one's earnings, eventually getting to the point where income from investments exceeds income from salaries. Many people think they are investing, but end up speculating instead. There are also those who think they can time the market and make quick money. These people are trading.

Investing is the allocation of funds in such a way that the odds are significantly on one's side. In speculating, the odds are slightly or moderately against your side. In trading, the odds are significantly against you.

For the gamblers out there, trading would be like placing large bets on single numbers in roulette – you can make some real money very quickly if your numbers pan out, but most of the time you will lose and quickly. Speculating is like playing on red and black or maybe on a third of the board at a time. You have a better chance of winning, but the odds are still against you and over time you will lose more than you win. Investing is like buying the casino, where now all of the odds are in your favor and you will, given time, win more than you lose. While the gambler may make a few quick wins and may sometimes walk away with more than he came in with, the casino owner will always win if he keeps playing (which is why they gladly give out free rooms to "winners").

In the stock market, trading involves doing things like buying a stock and then selling the same day if it goes up 1/4 point. There is an entire business built up around the process called *day trading,* in which individuals sit at their computers and make large trades on small movements in stocks. They will often trade a stock 10-20 times per day, making a dime or two at a time per share. Because they are trading 1000 or 2000 shares, they can make $100 or $200 dollars per trade. If they can do this many times a day, they can make $1000-$2000 or more each day, or $10,000-$20,000 per month.

While this may sound great, the trouble is they also lose money. On each of their successful trades they may make $50, paying $5-$10 of that in commissions. Each time they lose money, they also pay $5-$10 in commissions. Some studies have suggested that day traders need to have a return before expenses of 70% or more just to break even. Many day traders will regale you of the story where they made $10,000 in a single day. They will rarely tell you of all of the times they lost $3000, or even of the times they made money but paid it all out in commissions.

Speculating involves buying stocks and then selling within a few months to a year. Often speculating involves putting extremely large amounts of money (more than you'd be willing to lose) in a few stocks with the intention of selling and making a quick profit. Often speculators will sell winning positions and make a profit, but miss out on a truly significant run-up. For example, they might make a 10% profit in a few months, but miss out on a 200% profit they would have made if they had held the shares longer.

They may also get caught up in the mania and hold onto a hot stock for way too long, perhaps even buying more near the top because they start to believe the rise will continue forever. The Enron employees who had their entire retirement savings in Enron stock were speculating, although they probably did not realize it at the time.

In investing the odds are significantly in the favor of the investor. This is done primarily through the control of two factors, the holding period (time) and the type of stock selected. I will discuss each of these factors.

Time

A rule of statistics says that while there are short-term aberrations — a "lucky streak" or "unlucky streak" as the gambler would call it — if enough trials are performed, the result will always follow the odds. If a fair coin is tossed ten times, it may come out 9 times heads and 1 time tails, but if it is flipped 100 times or a million times the result will be about 50% heads and 50% tails. (Note that this is not the gambler's fallacy — the coin has no idea that it was heads 9 times out of 10, so the eleventh time is no more likely to be tails than it is to be heads. It is just that if the coin is flipped enough times, because there is an equal chance of heads or tails, there will be about as many heads as tails.)

If a random stock is bought for one day, there is about a 50-50 chance that it will go up, and a complimentary 50-50 chance that it will go down. If the market is going up it will probably go with it, but at the beginning of the day it is difficult to predict if the market will go up or down. The movement of an individual stock is not random, however — it is deterministic if all of the factors that influence its movement could be sensed and predicted. Likewise, the flip of a coin is not random — it could be predicted if all of the factors that influence its flight could be sensed and the effects predicted. But because there are so many factors, the behaviors of the coin and the stock over short periods of time appear random.

While it is not intuitive, the shorter the period of time, the more random seems a stock's behavior. If the movement is watched trade-by-trade, our eyes may pick out patterns (our minds are always trying to pick out patterns, even if none are there). We may therefore fool ourselves into thinking we can predict the next movement. If we counted the number of upticks and down-ticks over a suitable period of time (say two months), however, the number of upticks and down-ticks would be about 50-50, just like 1000 flips of the coin.

Watching CNBC or having the latest news via Twitter won't help either. Everybody receives the same news and as soon as you see the bad news, the price of the stock will have already fallen. Likewise, if good earnings come out, the price will shoot up before you can buy in. Information, provided that it is legally obtained, really doesn't help. The person on the other side of the trade will have heard the same news and changed the price accordingly.

For this reason, it is extremely difficult to figure out what the returns will be on stocks and other publicly traded assets during short periods of time. It is equally difficult to figure out which stocks will do well during any given year. It is reasonably easy, however, to figure out the long-term winners.

Investing in stocks is to buy and hold them for a long period of time – long enough to be able to predict with reasonable accuracy that the total return will be positive and high enough to be worth the risk taken. Investors don't pretend to know whether a stock will do well this month because they know all sorts of things can happen to the stock price during short periods of time. They just know that if they can find companies that will grow earnings over the next decade, the stock price will follow.

Looking at the longer term, however, predicting the behavior of stocks is like predicting the behavior of a coin. One could lay a bet with good confidence that the number of heads would lie between 400 and 600 if a coin is flipped 1000 times. I would not take a bet that a coin would be heads 4 to 6 times out of ten, but I would take one that it would be heads 400 to 600 times out of a thousand.

Likewise, one can predict with good confidence that the return of the market will be between 8 and 15% over a period of twenty or thirty years. For individual stocks, it is difficult to predict if a stock will be up or down in two months time, but one has good odds of predicting a stock will be up an average of about 15% per year if the earnings have been growing at 15% for the last several years and there is no reason to expect them to change. (Note that this is a long term average – the stock might be up 30% one year and then down 20% the next because of market conditions. It is just that if the stock is held long enough the average return would be about 15%.)

Obviously, this has its limits. It would be very difficult to determine which stocks around today will still be here in fifty years. Add enough time, and all sorts of things that cannot be foreseen may occur.

The goal therefore is to look far enough into the future to filter out the distortions caused by market fluctuations, but not so far so as to look beyond what can be reasonably predicted for corporate profits, growth, and so on. A stock should be purchased with the expectation that it will be held for a decade or more, but progress should be tracked periodically and changes made if things aren't working out as expected. Typically a review about once per year is sufficient.

Stock Selection
It is not simply enough to buy a stock at random, hold it for long periods of time, and then expect to do well. If one buys "the market" through the purchase of a set of mutual funds, one should expect to get the average market return, about 10-15%. To beat the market, one needs to select companies that will outperform their peers and the market. This is difficult to

do for short periods of time, but is not as difficult as one would think for long periods of time.

Perhaps the best way to go about stock selection is to think of buying a business rather than buying a stock. Rather than looking at price fluctuations, look at the current value of the company and its ability to grow more valuable. Would you buy a company that makes compact disk players when MP3 players are taking over the market? Would you buy something like Starbucks which is in every city in America or something like In-and-Out burger that has a strong Southern California following but few restaurants elsewhere?

Given this philosophy, here is how to put the odds in your favor, and invest rather than speculate:

1. Select companies where you can reasonably predict earnings and expect their earnings to continue to grow at a reasonable rate (10-15%) for the foreseeable future.

2. Determine the reasonable value for a company, based on current and future earnings, and buy companies that are trading in the low range of PE based on their history and that of their peers.

3. Invest for the long-term, riding out the random fluctuations caused by market effects. Use these effects to buy at discounts and sell at premiums.

4. Sell a stock only if 1) the company's business changes, such that it no longer has the characteristics for which you bought it, 2) the company becomes so overvalued, based on the historic PE ratio, that it would take years for the company's earnings to catch up with its price, or 3) the company has grown to the point where the prospects for future growth in earnings are dimming.

Serious Investing

In the previous section I discussed how the investor uses the factors of time and stock selection to reduce risk and put the odds in his favor. These factors can be used to great advantage by the individual investor, but sadly, few do so. It is because the individual investor can use time and stock selection to cut risk that he can lessen diversification without significantly increasing risk and thereby increase returns. This concept forms the basis for what I call *serious investing*, which is a central theme to this book and *The Small Investor Blog*.

The methodology behind serious investing will be presented in a later chapter, but the concept is introduced here. The idea behind serious investing is to concentrate investments into a few, best-of-breed stocks, and then hold these stocks for long periods of time.

The idea of concentration central to serious investing goes against traditional advice. Professional financial advisers will advise gobs and gobs of diversification. Some will swear off individual stocks entirely, saying they are too risky and that individual investors should stick to mutual funds. The goal here is to match the returns of the market, if possible.

It has been shown, however, that small investors can beat the market and the majority of professionals running mutual funds. The reason is that they have advantages over the professional managers which are utilized in the serious investing strategy. These are:

1) The small investor has the ability to concentrate positions. The large mutual fund manager can't concentrate in a few single stocks simply because there are not enough shares out there to do so, given how much money the professional funds manager has under management. The small investor can pick his favorite company in each sector and load up, while the professional manager must buy his favorite and five others. He also needs to buy only large, liquid stocks because he would move the price up if he were buying less liquid stocks. The small investor has no such limitation.

2) The small investor has the advantage of time. He does not need to sell to meet redemptions (people selling their shares of the mutual fund, forcing the manager to sell stocks to raise cash) when the market starts to fall and mutual fund investors start to pull their money out (at just the wrong moment). He does not need to make a high return each year to satisfy the investors. Also, he does not need to dress up his list of holdings at the end of each quarter to look like he chose all the winners — he can wait for the market to realize that the companies he's bought are gems.

The serious investor utilizes these advantages to outperform the market and the managers over time. He buys only the best. He buys in sufficient quantities so that when he picks a winner, he makes huge gains in his portfolio. And he doesn't pay attention to the market – he buys based on value and potential – and has the luxury of waiting for the market to price the stocks properly before selling.

At first the relative lack of diversification may seem risky, and it would be if not for the long-term strategy and the selection of suitable investments for the long-term. Many people start small businesses and pour everything they have into them and then some. In serious investing, you are providing capital to such entrepreneurs in exchange for a share of the profits if they are successful.

This is less risky than starting your own business because you are selecting businesses that already have shown some measure of success. You also get to take advantage of a team of highly trained managers who have come from the best business schools and/or proven themselves by moving up through the ranks. Finally, because you are buying a few stocks rather than starting a single business, you are spreading you investment over a hand-full of companies, all with great prospects.

Another reduction in risk comes from utilizing retirement accounts, such as 401k accounts, in addition to a taxable portfolio where the serious investing philosophy is put into practice. Because these accounts will be invested entirely in mutual funds, they offer a fallback position should your taxable portfolio not perform. Most people don't even take advantage of these accounts to the extent they should, so one who does so will be ahead of the game even before the investments in the taxable portfolio. Also, as time passes and account balances build, a portion of assets in the taxable account is shifted into mutual funds to provide diversification and to preserve the gains you've made.

The Relative Risk of Assets

Now that I have discussed the difference between investing and speculating, and discussed the use of time to reduce the risk posed by volatile assets, I'll revisit the various types of assets, this time to discuss the relative risk and potential reward of each. Risk and reward are often tied together, in that the greater the potential reward of an investment, the greater the risk that is being taken. There are prudent and even necessary risks to be taken in order to grow wealth and fight inflation, and then there are foolish risks that add entertainment value but rarely result in substantial gains over long periods of time. Serious investing is taking prudent risks. Speculating and trading are taking foolish risks.

As an aside, there is an additional type of assets that was not mentioned in the start of this chapter, and that is assets designed for *saving*. In saving, one accepts a very low rate of return, for example, in a money market fund, for high levels of liquidity and an almost assured return of one's money. If money is needed short-term, saving is appropriate. If funds are to be stored for long periods of time, investing in more volatile assets is needed to keep inflation from eroding value.

A partial list of the various instruments of saving, investment and speculation/trading, in rank from lowest risk to highest risk, would go something like this:

1. Cash, 2. Savings Account, 3. Money Market, 4. CDs, 5. Public Bonds, 6. Private Bonds, 7. Preferred Stocks, 8. Common Stocks, 9. Index Options, 10. Common Stock Options.

Typical rates of return for these options would be:

1-4 : (Bank Investments) Negative return after inflation, with cash doing the worst (-3-4%) and each option doing better with CD's having a negative rate of 1-2%
5-6: (Bonds) Return of 2-5% after inflation
7. (Preferred Stock) 5-6% after inflation
8. (Common Stocks) 6-12% after inflation
9-10. (Options) 30-100% or more after inflation.

Note that as risk increases, so does the possible return. The reason for this is that investors will not buy a product that carries significant risk unless it also carries a large return. If a bank is offering a 5-year CD, individuals will not put their money into it unless the rate is significantly above that offered by savings accounts. Likewise if a company wants to borrow money by issuing bonds, but the company has defaulted on their bonds in the past, investors won't buy the bonds unless the interest rate is high enough to justify the risk.

Items 1-4 are bank investments, which are insured not only by the soundness of the bank, but also by the backing of the Federal Government. When one puts money into these types of investments, the amount of return is directly specified and very rarely is the return promised not attained. The only difference in rate is based on the length of the loan to the bank and the liquidity of the money. In the case of bank investments, the higher interest rates for longer term loans (*e.g.* 5-year CDs) are tied to the non-availability of the funds rather than due to any increased risk, since it is very rare that a bank CD would not be repaid in full.

Items 5-6, bonds, have more risk that bank investments since it is more common for companies and municipalities to default on bonds. When that occurs the bond holder is put in line with other creditors to recover whatever they can of the loan that was made. Typically they will receive 10-20 cents on the dollar or some nearly worthless shares of stock when defaults occur. Bonds are therefore priced based upon the perceived risk that the government entity or the company will default on the loan. This is based on the company or municipality's finances and past history, just like a personal loan.

Bonds are loans made for fixed periods of time, after which time the money invested by the bond holder is repaid in full (if the company is able). In other words, even though the price of a bond may fluctuate over the life of the bond, when the bond's expiration date comes, the bondholder can expect to receive the par value, typically $1000 per bond. For this reason bonds are more predictable and therefore less risky than preferred and common stocks, items 7 and 8.

Both preferred and common stocks continue indefinitely and there is no agreement to return the original investment of the buyer. Preferred stocks, item 7, are more risky than bonds but less risky than common stocks since they pay good dividends and investors in preferred shares are paid dividends before holders of common stock. They are also in line before common stock holders in the event of a bankruptcy, not that either party is likely to get anything. Most of the return from common stocks is due to appreciation in price. This occurs when the value of the company grows, which can be unpredictable, so common stocks are more risky than bonds or preferred stocks.

Items 9-10, options, are too risky to be called investments. These assets are pure speculations since the odds are clearly against the buyer. Not only must one be right about the direction of the price of the underlying stock, but one must be right about the time frame in which that move will occur. Options expire worthless after a specified period of time, so even if you are right and the stock goes up 2000%, if the move occurs one year later and your options expire after 3 months, you would lose your entire position.

As stated, the possible return on an investment depends on the risk taken. The reason is that individuals (wise individuals) would not make an investment or even a speculation unless the potential payout justified the risk. In the next section, I'll discuss what is called the *risk premium*.

Asset Pricing and the Risk Premium

An important concept to understand in investing is risk versus return, often expressed as a risk/reward ratio. The basic idea is that the risk/reward ratio should be about the same for any investment. If an investor is taking more risk, he should expect to have the chance to get a greater return on his investment. This additional return is called the *risk premium*, since the investor must receive a premium in the amount of potential reward before committing funds.

For example, a bank account is a fairly risk-free investment. Because losses in banks are very rare — even rarer since the Government began insuring bank accounts and requiring that banks hold a certain amount of capital in reserve — the amount of return from a bank account is fairly low. Bank investors do not expect a large return from their savings accounts as long as they can reasonably expect to be able to get the money back when they need it. They mainly put the money in the bank to keep it safe from thieves and their own spending. As stated in the last section, the return is actually a little worse than inflation, in fact, so wise investors only keep as much in savings accounts as they may need in the near future.

Investing in common stocks carries a bit more risk. There is always a chance that a company's business strategy may not work, or that someone in a company may make a big mistake, or that the company will get sued, causing a large loss. Even if nothing big happens, company earnings may not grow as expected and the share price may stagnate, resulting in an opportunity cost — money invested in a company that goes nowhere instead of another stock that grows. For these reasons investors will not put money into stocks unless there is an opportunity to make significantly better returns than in a bank account. Because stocks have historically had better returns than bank accounts, and are one of the few ways to beat inflation over long periods of time, investors have continued to put money into stocks.

As said at the start of this section, the risk/reward ratio for different investments tends to be nearly constant. For example, if the risk of investing in a bank account is 1 (some arbitrary unit), and it's return is 2%, the risk/reward ratio is 1/2 or 0.5. If a common stock investment is five times as risky as the bank account, one should not invest in the stock unless the potential rate of return is at least five times as much. The risk/reward ratio would then be 5/10 = 0.5, just as with the bank deposit.

Luckily for the investor, there is little need to actually calculate risk and return when investing in stocks. The pricing of common stocks tends to reflect this automatically since the prices are set through an auction system in which the bidders take the current levels of risk and reward into account. If bank account yields increase, the price of common stocks would tend to fall. Because the return from a bank account is then higher, the potential return from common stocks must also be greater, so investors bid down the price until the ratio of the current price to the expected price in the near future is sufficient to account for the risk.

When choosing whether or not to make an investment in a particular asset, the potential reward should be taken into account. This is the reason to avoid day trading. As discussed previously, in day trading investors buy stocks for short periods of time, often selling if very small gains (1/8 point or less) are made. The chance of a trade going the investor's way over a short period of time, however, is about 50-50, so the chance of losing money is equal to the chance of making money.

 Since the potential gains are very small, because positions are closed when small gains are made, the rewards are very limited. The risks are substantially greater than investing in a bank account, however. Therefore, the risk/reward ratio of day trading is not sufficient. Over time, one would do much better just leaving his money in the bank than day trading.

The serious investing strategy – investing in carefully selected common stocks and holding for long periods of time–certainly carries more risk than investing in a bank account. Risk is reduced, however, by the careful selection of stocks (companies that have successful business models and should be expected to continue to grow) and the long-term horizon (so that the effects of market distortions do not matter). In addition, the profit potential is substantial. Long-term investments of a few thousand dollars have turned into millions of dollars with companies such as Microsoft and Wal-mart. For this reason, the risk/reward ratio is very favorable.

Having covered the risk premium and gone into the relative risk of various assets, we now turn to a more in-depth discussion of the main assets suitable for investing: stocks, bonds, and real estate. For those still tempted to try a bit of speculation (hopefully with money you don't mind losing), I'll then talk about the specific risks of options and other speculative instruments.

Risk and Reward of Common Stocks

When looking at different investing options, there are many choices that are safer than common stocks, including savings accounts, money market funds, government savings bonds, treasury bonds, paid-for real estate, municipal and corporate bonds, and preferred stocks. When buying common stocks, one is taking an ownership stake in a company. Most of the profit that is made comes from the value of the company increasing, which is reflected in the increase in the price of the stock. If that company does well, one will prosper. If it does poorly, the price of the stock may drop or it may just trade within a range for years and never go anywhere. In the latter case, one would have been better off investing in bonds since at least there would have been a steady return from the interest payments.

When investing in stocks short-term, there are also risks related to the way the price is set. While illegal, there are various people and groups who manipulate stock prices from time to time. Because they are forward looking, stock prices may also move in unpredictable ways even when there is no manipulation. For example, if there is a rumor that a company may have good earnings, the stock may move up in price. When the earnings come out, even if there are record earnings, the price may drop if they are not as high as the marketplace was expecting.

A final risk of common stocks, since one is investing in a business, is that there may be some event which causes great damage to the company. Examples include fraud by the officers, lawsuits by customers or others, and new regulations and government actions (for example, the government moratorium on drilling in the Gulf after the TransOcean/BP oil spill). These can cause the price of a stock to drop dramatically and can even cause a company to go out-of-business very quickly.

Despite stocks being more risky than many investment options, there are good reasons to invest mainly in the stock market *for long-term holdings*. They are one of the few ways to beat inflation, require little maintenance and never require additional cash (like real estate), and allow for tax-deferred compounding so long as the shares are not traded frequently. Stocks therefore should hold a prominent place in the portfolio of the long term investor.

Risk and Rewards of Bonds

As first explained in Chapter 2, a bond is a loan made to a company (or government entity). Just as with a house loan, the loan is made for a specified period of time. Unlike a house loan, however, the loan is not repaid over time with the amount owed decreasing each year. Instead, the company will pay a fixed amount of interest on the loan during the period and then repay the loan all at once at the end. For example, a bond with a *par value* (loan value) of $1000 and a coupon of 5% would pay $50 per year, or $25 every six months. When the bonds mature, the person holding the bonds would be paid $1000 plus the final $25 interest payment.

During the life of the bond, it will be freely traded on the market and the price will fluctuate. An advantage is that one can make both interest and a capital gain from bonds. For example, if an investor bought the bond listed above when it was trading for $500 and then held it to maturity, he would receive both the interest payments, at an effective rate of 10% for him, and $1000 when the bond matured. He would therefore make a $500 capital gain in addition to the interest he earned.

While it varies by company and term, bonds are generally safer than stocks. The reasons are that the bond pays a fixed interest amount, meaning that a return is generated even if stock prices are going nowhere. Also, no matter what the price of the bond does during its lifetime, one can hold the bond to maturity and receive the full $1000 face amount. As with anything, however, there are risks. Here are the main risks of corporate bonds:

Default: Obviously the primary risk with a bond is that the company that issues the bond will be unable to pay and will therefore default on the bond. When this occurs, sometimes the company will issue shares of stock to repay part of the loan, sometimes the company will repay the loan but at a later date, and sometimes the company will just default and not pay. In general when a company defaults on a bond the investor should expect to get little or nothing back.

Interest Rate Rises: Because bonds are primarily bought for the interest they pay, they are very sensitive to changes in interest rates. For example, if banks start paying higher interest rates, because a bank account is less risky than a bond, many investors will sell their bonds and invest their money in the bank. Because of this, the price of bonds will decrease, causing the interest rates they pay to increase (remember that bond interest rates go in the opposite direction of the price of the bond). Buying bonds at periods like the present time, where interest rates are rock bottom and only likely to go up, is especially risky. On the other hand, buying bonds when interest rates are very high and most likely to go down is a sound strategy. As interest rates decrease the price of the bond will go up. This will provide capital gains income in addition to the relative high interest rate that will be locked in when buying the bond.

Early Call: If interest rates are sufficiently low many bonds will trade above their par value. This is because investors will go to bonds in order to increase the amount of interest they make when bank accounts are paying nothing. Many companies have call provisions that allow them to repay the bonds early if they are trading above par value. If interest rates are very low they may well call the bonds, paying the par value, and then issue new bonds at a lower rate. This is much like a person refinancing their home. When this happens, if you've bought at above par value, you will lose the difference between the price you paid and par value.

Risk and Reward of Real Estate

Real estate has always been seen as a low risk investment. Houses always go up in value, people say. Sometimes prices might stall for a while or not grow that fast, but they will always pick up again. You may need to just sit pat for a while and wait for the market to recover. Buying a home has also provided a fairly good return. This is if one forgets about all of the upkeep expenses and the property taxes paid each year.

For many the home has also been the retirement plan. As discussed in the last chapter, most people would have essentially no retirement savings unless the company they worked for provided a pension when they were ready to retire. Because the house was paid off, however, they were able to sell the big house where the kids were raised and move to a small condo, using the rest of the money for living expenses. The gains on the home's value were even tax-free unless the home was above a certain value. Unfortunately, the latest generation nearing retirement have been taking out so many loans on their homes, getting a new loan for a kitchen upgrade or a vacation each time the value increased, that instead of having home equity to use for retirement they'll have a set of mortgage and home equity loan payments to pay well into their nineties.

Before the 2008 fall in real estate prices, many believed that houses could not decline in value, at least not by much. Declines of 5-15% had been seen here and there, but certainly not 30-40% declines. The thought was that one should take out a huge loan and buy all of the home one could. As it went up in value, you would gain on the equity. You could even take the equity out through a home equity loan or by refinancing and pay for college, a new car, or that trip you've been wanting to take.

Until the collapse, many did not realize the risk inherent in buying a home with a huge mortgage. The reason that individuals could put a few thousand dollars (or maybe nothing) into a home and sell it a year or two later and make tens of thousands of dollars was that they were dealing in huge amounts of leverage. For a down payment of $5,000, or no down payment at all, one could buy a $500,000 house — you were multiplying the purchasing power of that $5,000 one hundred to one! If the housing market went up just 5% that year, you could make $25,000, or a 500% gain. If you had bought the house for cash instead, you would have only seen a 5% gain, and most of that would have been due to inflation. It is the large amount of leverage employed that causes the outsized gains.

But as anyone who has even dealt with leverage will tell you, it can cause substantial losses of money you don't have when things go South. If that same house went down just 5%, you would now owe $20,000 more than the price for which you could sell the house. The person who had trouble scraping together the $5,000 down payment and was barely able to make the monthly payment now would need to come up with $20,000 from somewhere if he wanted to sell the house.

This was not a big deal if the person was planning to stay in the home, but throw in a job loss and you see someone trapped by leverage in an area with no jobs. To make matters even worse, many of the loans were adjustable rate, meaning that the initial low teaser rates were replaced with higher rates, resulting in an increase in the monthly payment. Because many of the people who took out these loans could only afford the low teaser rate, they were unable to keep paying the mortgage payments after the rates reset, even if they kept their jobs.

This resulted in a foreclosure or a short sale, which drove prices down further, putting other home purchasers under water, and the cycle continued. In some cases individuals decided it was unfair that they should have to continue to pay for their mortgage if the house was not worth the current loan value, so they simply stopped paying the mortgage, driving prices down further. Hence the current financial meltdown.

The point is not that people shouldn't buy houses – it is definitely good to get to the point where you own your house outright and don't need to worry about a rent payment.

Buying real estate as an investment is also a good way to smooth out one's portfolio since real estate often moves in a manner uncorrelated with the stock market. When stocks go down, house prices may go up or at least remain about the same, and rents will usually continue to come in.

The point is to understand the leverage involved in real estate loans and to minimize the amount of leverage used, and thereby to lower risk and avoid being trapped. In buying one's own home, here are some wise choices to make:

1) Make as big a down payment as possible. 100% down is not a bad plan. If you can't manage that, at least give yourself enough of a cushion so as to not be trapped in the house if prices decline.

2) Take out as short term a loan as you can. Ideally you should have the house paid off before the kids are ready for college. Try to obtain a 15-year loans or less. This will save tens of thousands of dollars in the actual amount paid for the home. The interest rate will also be lower.

3) Home mortgage payments should not exceed 25% of your take-home pay. This is a manageable amount. A bigger loan increases risk of default should something happen to your income stream and will generally not leave you much flexibility from month-to-month because your free cash flow will be so small. Even if you have the disposable income to make the payments, a large mortgage will reduce your ability to save for retirement and obtain other goals.

4) Consider starting out with a smaller home and trading up. Remember that your parents didn't start their first job and buy a 4000 square foot McMansion. They probably started small and worked their way up. If you can, start in a small house early when you don't need much space (and could use the

extra time working rather than cleaning house or doing yard work), work hard to pay it off, and then trade up in house with a big down payment from the sale of the smaller house. Doing so will allow you to buy more home for less since the amount you pay in interest will be reduced.

5) Always use a fixed rate loan. With a adjustable rate mortgage, the interest rate will always reset at the worst possible moment. And with rates currently at all time lows, in which direction would you expect them to reset?

High Risk/High Reward Speculations

Other types of securities or trades carry so much risk that they can no longer be thought of as investments. It is impossible to get the odds sufficiently on your side. Therefore they can be thought of as speculations at best, and gambles at worst. The least risky of these speculations are discussed below.

Short Sales

A short sale is the exact opposite of the purchase of a stock, in that an investor makes money when the stock goes down in price and loses money if it goes up. In a short sale an investor borrows shares of a company and sells them, collecting the proceeds from the sale. At a later date he purchases shares on the open market, thereby replacing the shares that were borrowed and closing the transaction. The shares are sold first, then bought later. Like a normal stock purchase, money is made when they sell for more than the purchase price.

Some of the terminology of short sales:

Cover: To buy back shares that were sold short, closing the transaction.

Buy Long: To buy stocks or other securities in the normal fashion, such that increases in price result in profits.

Naked Short: A trade in which the shares are not borrowed before being sold short. This is an illegal transaction because it can allow for a great deal of shares to be sold short that don't exist, upsetting the balance between buyers and sellers, causing price manipulation.

Short and Ultrashort ETF: Funds designed to go down when the underlying index goes up, with equal percentages on a day-to-day basis. These are typically not recommended.

Despite looking like a standard stock trade, but done in reverse, there are some special nuances that must be understood about short sales. These are:

Tax Implications: Short sales are always considered short-term trades, no matter how long they are held open, probably because short selling is considered somehow sinister or evil. (Disclaimer: Note that as with all tax information offered in this book, this statement should be checked with a CPA since I am not one and could be wrong. Tax laws also change all of the time.)

Time Frame: Short sales are inherently short to mid-term investments. Because the tendency of the stock market is to increase in price, time works against the short sale. Going short a stock and then forgetting about it is not a good strategy. For this reason, selling short is more speculation than investment.

Risk: It is often said that short selling is more risky than buying long because your loss is limited when buying long (the stock can only go to zero), while a stock can go up forever. While this is technically true, the risk is manageable because stocks don't go up infinite amounts as long as the investor is very disciplined and has a firm price target above which she will cover and close the transaction, no matter what. If the company is bought out or other big news occurs, the stock may shoot right through the target, but even then stocks don't just go from $10 to $500 in a day. Still, because time works against the short sale to some extent, there is more risk in selling short than going long.

Effect of bad positions: If one buys long and a stock goes down, while a loss is being taken, the position becomes a smaller and smaller percentage of the portfolio as the stock declines. With short selling, if the stock goes up, the position becomes larger and larger, becoming a bigger portion of the portfolio. Also, if a loss is taken on a short sale, money must be found to pay for brokerage commissions in addition to the loss, where with selling at a loss on a long position the money gained from the trade will at least cover the brokerage costs.

Margin Interest: While a stock is sold short, it is a liability against the account. If there is not as much cash in the account as the value of the short sale, the investor will need to pay margin interest on the difference (which is where financial firms actually make their money). If the stock price rises far enough, a margin call can be executed that will force the investor to cover the position and lose substantial amounts. Also, the cash kept in the account to cover the value of the short sale will not receive interest (it is held against the short sale).

As can be seen, there are many specific risks and disadvantages with short sales; therefore, they should be seen as a speculation, not an investment. Still, there are sometimes when selling short makes sense.

The time when it may be worth selling short is when the market is so unbelievably over-valued, or the likelihood of the market falling is so great (like in the summer of 2008), that stocks in general, or at least in a certain sector, are much more likely to fall than to rise. Even in this case short selling is done only as a hedge for long positions – trying to offset losses in long positions by going short on other stocks.

For example, in the summer of 2008 the housing bubble was threatening to burst. I owned a lot of retailer stocks that I knew would be hurt if consumers were no longer able to roll their credit card balances into their home loans, but I did not want to sell the stocks outright. I decided therefore that shorting some of the home lenders would be a good hedge. My goal was to gain money from the short sales to offset the temporary losses on the long positions I held.

Since the home lenders had been doing very well and the price of their shares had risen a lot over the past few years, I reasoned that their stocks were not likely to go much higher unless I was very wrong about their earnings prospects. I also felt that they would get hit hard when the ARMs reset and people stopped being able to make their payments. At least, I thought, that the number of new loans they would be making – which is where they made most of their money – would decrease, causing their stock price to fall since earnings would no longer be growing at their previous, torrid pace. I therefore took up short positions in several lenders.

I also saw that oil prices were very high, and that the price of oil stocks was probably as high as it would get. I thought that if the economy slowed down, demand for gasoline would fall. Because the shares were already at high prices, I reasoned that they were unlikely to go a great deal higher. I therefore went short several refinery stocks.

Even though I was eventually right in taking the short positions and did very well in 2009 while most investors were taking large losses, it was not uneventful. Shortly after I took up a short position in Golden West Financial, the stock was bought out, jumping from about $20 to the mid-thirties in a day. Eventually Golden West Financial gave great heart burn to the company that acquired them. I was right about the future of Golden West's business, but that was of little solace to me because I had already lost quite a bit on the trade when the company was acquired (I had a similar experience with shorting Snapple).

So to sum things up, short selling can be profitable, but the interim movements of the stock you are shorting can cause losses, even if you are eventually right about the company. Also, just because a stock is very expensive doesn't mean it can't go higher for a while or that another company might not buy it out for even more money. I therefore only sell short when I believe there are systemic risks in the market and I wish to hedge against a fall rather than selling outright. I also only short stocks that I believe have gone up so much that they have a lot more room on the downside than the upside.

Options, LEAPS, and Warrants:

Options, LEAPS, and warrants are all derivatives, which means that they derive their value from the value of some other equity. Derivatives by their nature use a great deal of leverage, and therefore are extremely risky. In particular, all of these types of assets are wasting assets, meaning that their value declines with time. Not only do you need to be right, but you need to be right within a certain amount of time. If the stock doubles in price the day before expiration of your options, you may make a fortune. If it doubles the day after, you lose the entire position.

In general none of these types of securities are suitable for an investor. Investors buy stakes in companies and hold them for long periods of time – they don't play short term price swings. If one is looking for a little excitement and the casinos aren't appealing, a small amount (say 5% of a portfolio) might be used for such speculations. Plan on losing the entire position, however, since that is precisely what will often happen.

There are some valid times to use options, however. Options were designed to be used as insurance. By buying a put option on a large amount of stock, for example, one could put a floor on the price at which the stock could be sold. Perhaps if one thought the price was way to high but wanted to delay the sale into the next year for tax purposes, one might buy a put option to lock in the gain without selling the stock and realizing the gain in the current tax year. Like all insurance, however, by buying a put you are insuring that you will lose at least the cost of the premium. It is often more efficient to simply sell the shares to lock in the gain.

Chapter 4
Matching Investment Risk to Stage in Life

Having covered the specific risks of different types of investments in Chapter 3, we now look at matching asset selection and investment style to stage in life. While one can certainly start investing at any stage of life, the style that is appropriate is tied both to one's age and income status. A twenty-year old who has a steady job and is looking to grow wealth has a different objective and risk tolerance than an individual in her late fifties who would like to retire in a few years. It therefore makes sense that the investment strategy should change with stage of life.

Ideally one starts investing at about the time she starts working. This will provide the best chance for obtaining financial independence – that state where one is fully self-sufficient without any outside income. There are specific investing stages that one would go through starting from the start of one's working career. These are as discussed in the sections that follow.

If the reader is in his mid to late career and has not already amassed a good sum of wealth, he will be starting at a disadvantage in the game. The risks that you can take early in a career and those that a person staring down the barrel of retirement can accept are different. Those starting later can still use the plan as a guide, however, just starting from the stage of life one is in. You would just need to increase diversification more to reduce risk since you wouldn't have as many years to recover from a financial loss. Understand, however, that you must start early to fully use the power of compounding interest. Some of this can be overcome by drastic saving and investing later in life, particularly with a large income, but it is far easier if one starts young.

Before discussing the investment strategy appropriate for each life stage, an understanding of the factors that affect risk and return for an investment is needed. These factors are volatility, diversification, and time frame. The young investor can take more volatility and diversification risk because she can reduce risk through her investment time frame. The older investor must protect assets by lowering volatility and increasing diversification. First, we will discuss volatility.

Note that in Chapter 3 investment risk was discussed in terms of time and asset selection. Time is related to time frame, and asset selection is related to volatility and diversification. In this chapter we therefore look at risk in a slightly different, but nonetheless consistent way.

Volatility
Investing in stocks and bonds is not like putting money in a bank account where one can calculate the interest rate and know the value at a future point in time. Stocks and other assets go up and down in price and one cannot predict what price they will be at one year, one month, or even a few days in the future. The level of these fluctuations varies with the asset type and the specific investment.

The size and frequency of these seemingly random motions is called *volatility* and is often described by a quantity called an investment's *beta*. Basically, a beta of 1.0 means that the asset has an equal volatility to the average asset in the market. Higher values of beta indicate that it will move around a lot more. The stocks of young companies and companies in industries like semiconductors and biotechs tend to have high betas. As can be expected, the price of these assets varies wildly from month-to-month.

Studies have shown that stocks with higher betas will do well over long periods of time. This is because those individuals buying higher beta stocks are taking on more risk, and therefore these stocks tend to be priced to provide a higher return than a low beta stock. Stocks in general have higher levels of volatility than some other investments, which increases risk. It is specifically because of this risk, however, that one can make returns that are much better than bank rates.

The potential return on an investment is proportional to the volatility. In Chapter 2 a list of popular investment choices was presented in order from least risky to most risky. Let's return to a similar list of assets and examine these choices in terms of volatility. As will be seen, the assets types that were the most risky also tend to have the highest volatility.

Of the popular investments, a list of the least volatile/lowest return to the most volatile/highest return would be as follows:

1. Savings Account
2. Money Market
3. US Treasury
4. Bank CD
5. Investment Grade Bond
6. Preferred Stock
7. Large Company Common Stock
8. Junk Bonds
9. Hard Commodities (gold, silver, platinum)
10. LEAPs and Warrants
11. Options

Bank accounts and CDs are not volatile – the rate of interest is easily calculated such that the value at any given time will be known. The price of a "share" in a savings account does not fluctuate – a dollar invested can be redeemed at any time for a dollar. There is a slight risk that the bank may close and not be able to repay the money — a risk that was reduced after FDIC insurance program was started — but most of the time the interest is paid as expected. With all bank cash assets one is able to ask for the money back at any time, albeit at times with the forfeiture of some interest.

With stocks and bonds, the value of the investment fluctuates with time. One can not be certain what the value will be tomorrow or the next day, or even next year – it is whatever someone is willing to pay for the stock or bond at the time. Because bonds mature, meaning that the company that issues them will pay back the original loan at some date, they tend to be less risky. If the company issuing them, however, is shaky and likely to default, as is the case with junk bonds, the stock of a stable company would be less risky because one only risks loss of a portion of one's investment if the stock declines in price rather than a loss of the whole investment, which occurs when a company defaults on a bond.

For a stock one can assume that the price will be close to where it was the day before; however, significant news — good or bad — can cause the price to move by 10% or more in a day. Sometimes a stock will rise or fall for reasons that have nothing to do with the company. The whole market will move due to word of recession, war, pending legislation, or other events. Sometime it is just movements of the stock prices themselves or various trading strategies that are being employed by others in the market that will cause a stock price to move precipitously. This effect has become more prevalent with the invention of automated trading.

It is this volatility, however, that makes stocks grow more over time and provide a greater return than safer, fixed income investments. Because there is risk involved, one is able to buy stocks at significant discounts to what the earnings prospects of the company indicate the price will be. Because the company may not make the earnings that are expected, and later pay the dividends that come from such earnings, the price

68

of a stock will drop until it is low enough to justify the risk taken. If earnings and stock prices could be predicted more reliably, the risk premium, as discussed previously, would be lower.

Diversification

It is uncommon for single stocks to drop in value by half or more over short periods of time, but it certainly can happen. If a scandal breaks out or a large lawsuit occurs, a company may go bankrupt in a period of days. For this reason it is not a good idea to put more into a single position than one is willing to lose. Probably the worst thing a person can do is invest all of one's money in shares of the company for which one works. In that case if the company has sudden financial problems, or the CEO gets indicted, you can lose your job and your investments in one day (see Enron).

To reduce the risk of a substantial loss due to an event happening to any one security, one uses *diversification*. Diversification is the spreading out of one's money over several stocks, asset types, and even regions or countries. By buying several different assets, the effect on a portfolio of a dramatic price decline in one asset due to some random event affecting just that asset will be limited. For example, if you own 10 different stocks in equal amounts, you can only lose 10% due to an event occurring with any individual stock, even if the price of that one stock drops to zero.

Note that this also works when prices go the other way. By buying more than one stock, you increase the chances of buying one that will be the next Microsoft and increase a thousand percent or more. A balance must be struck, however, between buying enough different stocks/assets to provide sufficient protection and yet still buying enough of each asset to provide a good return. If you bought Microsoft in the 1980's but only bought 10 shares because you were diversified over several stocks in a mutual fund, you would still have made only a few thousand dollars despite the huge increase in share price. If you had instead bought 1000 shares in Microsoft, due to concentration you would be a multi-millionaire today. The amount of diversification appropriate depends on you stage in life, asset balance, and personal risk tolerance.

If you buy a sufficient number of different stocks, or buy a few mutual funds, you will get about the return of the stock market, which generally ranges between about -10% and +15% in a year, but can see swings of between -50% and +100% during extreme years. During the Great Depression, the market fell by 90%, but then proceeded to rally back, increasing tenfold (1000%) in the years that followed. In 2008 stocks fell by about 50%, but then rallied back within the next two years, regaining all of the lost value. During the bear market of 2011, we saw shares fall by about 15%.

If one includes different asset types beyond stocks (like bonds), one will get a return that is the weighted average of the different assets purchased. For example, if one had a portfolio of 50% bonds and 50% stocks, and stocks returned 15% and bonds returned 7% over a ten-year period, the total return for the portfolio would be 11%, which is less than the return for a portfolio consisting of only stocks. During down markets, however, the declines in bonds tend to be less than those for stocks, so the 50-50 portfolio would be safer than the 100% stock portfolio. Remember that getting greater returns always requires taking more risk.

While diversification into several different stocks reduces the effects of a bad event at any one company, it does not reduce *market risk.* Market risk is the chance that the entire market

70

will decline, taking good stocks with bad down with it. For example, in the period of 2007-2008, most stocks declined by 50% or more. Even if one had 10 different stocks, one still would have had a large negative return for the period.

To reduce market risk, one needs to buy *uncorrelated assets* or negatively *correlated assets*. The former are assets that move independently of each other, for example, stocks in Chinese companies and real estate in Seattle. The latter are assets that normally move opposite to each other. Obviously one will never make much of a return by buying negatively correlated assets since gains in one group will always be offset by losses in the other, but it is a good way to preserve wealth for short periods of time.

As shown above with our example stock/bond portfolio, diversification reduces risk, but it also lowers returns. Too much diversification when one is just starting out in investing and has little money to invest will limit the rate of growth. Your $2,000 initial investment will probably be worth less than $3,000 in ten years if you bought several stock and bond mutual funds (if you could make investments in several funds with such a low minimum balance). That rate of return is fine if you have several hundred thousand dollars and want to get modest growth while preserving what you have. When you are starting with very little capital, however, and have a long time horizon (see the next section) that allows you to recover from mistakes, it makes sense to use less diversification.

Another disadvantage of diversification is that money is not put into only the best places. With heavy diversification, one needs to buy both favorite stocks and less-than-favorite stocks. When one is trying to grow wealth, it makes sense to concentrate in what one thinks will be the winners. As one's net worth builds, one then begins to worry more about return *of* capital than return *on* capital; therefore, diversification should increase as one shifts from trying to increase wealth while young to trying to maintain wealth when older.

Time Frame

The third concept affecting risk and return, which is often ignored by financial planners, is time frame. Time frame is the amount of time an investment is expected to be held. The purchase of high volatility assets would be nothing more than gambling if one were planning to invest for a few months or a few weeks. Likewise, buying lots of shares of a single stock for a short period of time is very risky.

To understand why, one must understand the components that make up the price of a stock. A stock's price has a deterministic, fundamental price component and a non-deterministic, random component. The fundamental price, which is the predictable part of a stock's price, is set based on current earnings, business prospects, the state of the economy, politics, and other factors. On top of the fundamental price are seemingly random fluctuations due to the effects of various trading strategies, investor emotions, and things unrelated to the company going on in the investors' lives.

The price of a stock at any given time factors in all of the current news, so changes in price are due to the random component, which is based on guesses of those trading shares at the time. Unless you are trading illegally on insider information (or are a member of Congress and trading legally on insider information) you will never hear a story first and sell or buy shares before the price changes to reflect the news. It therefore makes no sense to buy or sell a stock due to the news that comes out – it is already priced into the stock.

Because short-term changes are only due to random effects, it is difficult to predict price over short periods of time, between one and three years. The random component of a share price can be as large or larger than the fundamental component, and therefore the price for shares presented by the market are not necessarily rational at any given time. Stocks that are overpriced can continue to rise. Those that are dirt cheap can get cheaper. Often this is due to investor emotions – one who sees a stock's price going up may buy because he is expecting to sell for more later. One who has lost money may sell at a low price to just get out, and others may not buy for fear of seeing the price drop further. It is much easier to predict stock prices over long periods of time because the price will eventually follow the fundamentals – the random portion is just a ripple on top of the fundamental price, like an eddy in a river.

Even if one buys shares in a great company, the general market sentiment can cause the price to fall and stay down for short periods of time. There is also manipulation, various trading strategies, and all kinds of random events that can affect prices over the short term. Maybe you'll buy that great stock and then the founder will decide to unload a bunch of shares and buy a house.

Even a stock's fundamental price does not typically change immediately due to the expected future return. For example, a stock's price will not necessarily double in price if earnings five years down the road are expected to double. The reason is that there is risk involved in the company actually achieving the expected earnings. The current price is less than, or *discounted* relative to the expected future price, to reward the investor sufficiently for taking on the additional risk.

It is fortunate for an investor that the fundamental price of a stock does not instantly reflect predicted future earnings since that provides an opportunity for profiting through long-term investing. It is due to this discount, which is proportional to the risk being undertaken, that stocks do better than most assets over long periods of time. Because the returns are greater when companies actually do meet earnings targets, you will do better buying a diversified set of stocks than you will buying a diversified set of bonds. In addition, stocks have a natural tendency to rise as the economy grows and earnings increase. Returns on stocks over long periods of time have averaged between ten and fifteen percent — much better rates than those of most other investments.

One way to lesson the effects of random variations is to buy shares regularly, rather than putting all of one's money in at once. This lessens the effects of market fluctuations since more shares are bought while prices are low than when they are high. This process, called "dollar cost averaging," is a popular and effective technique.

So the allocation of assets into bank accounts, bonds, stocks, real estate, and other investments is highly dependent on time frame. For those with only a few years to invest, the money should be safely invested in a bank CD despite the terrible interest rates since there will not be enough time for inflation to deflate the value too much. For those who are saving for retirement and have decades to let the money grow, the money must be in assets with more return than the bank. Otherwise inflation will decrease the actual value of the account each year since the bank cash rate of return is always a little less than the rate of inflation.

So to summarize, volatility increases risk but also increases potential return. Diversification decreases risk by reducing the effect any one asset can have on total portfolio value, but also reduces potential return to that of the market. Increases in time frame reduce risk since assets tend to increase in value with time, time allows assets that have fallen in value to recover, and it is much easier to predict which assets will do well over longer periods of time than shorter ones. These three factors are used together when developing an investment strategy suited for stage of life and risk tolerance.

The Strategy for a Life-Long Investment Plan

Having discussed the basics of investing and the factors that affect risk and the potential return, we will now use these factors over the next several chapters to lay out a lifelong investment strategy. This strategy assumes that you begin investing when you first start your first job and continue throughout your life. Used effectively, the strategy can allow the individual investor to beat the mutual fund manager and even the average returns of the general market.

Now, note that few investors or even mutual fund managers beat the market. The average mutual fund will provide the same rate of return as the market, minus a few percentage points due to fees and trading expenses. Most investors don't do even as well as the mutual fund managers, even if they spend a lot of time studying stocks, trading shares, and trying to nimbly jump in and out of stocks in the nick of time.

As stated when the concept of serious investing was introduced, the strategy needed to beat the market and the average mutual fund differs from the standard advice for small investors that favors large amounts of diversification from the very start regardless of age. Some advisers will even recommend against investing in common stocks directly at all because they believe sufficient diversification cannot be achieved without mutual funds. For them one must be invested in thousands of different stocks in every sector of the market. A good portion must also be invested in bonds and other income securities, even when you are in your thirties and decades away from retirement.

And yet thousands of people start their own business and succeed each year. In that case they are betting on one company – theirs. This would be extremely risky for an individual who is nearing retirement and needs to succeed to eat. When one is young and has a long time frame, however, that time frame gives enough time to wait for businesses to grow and succeed. Likewise, that long time frame allows for one to recover when things do not work out when investing in stocks. It therefore makes sense to use less diversification and only buy the best companies while one has a longer time frame, and switch to a more diversified approach as personal wealth grows.

The strategy also doesn't involve trying to time the market or spot trends in the price patterns of stocks. It has been shown that timing simply doesn't work. The reason is that while the average rate of return from the markets is between 10-15%, most of the gains are had during very brief periods of time. If one tries to time the market, jumping in and out, one may very well miss one of the significant moves upwards.

Instead, the serious investing strategy is to buy large interests in companies with good prospects for substantial growth in the years ahead while one is young and has a long time horizon. In doing so, one is acting like a silent partner in these companies, providing capital needed for the managers to grow the business. This is as opposed to trading stocks, where one is trying to pick the stock whose price will go up soon, or simply buying the market through a diversified set of mutual funds.

The random component in the price of a stock will always be there. The price of the shares of these companies should be expected to rise and fall with the economy and various market pressures. By investing in the company as a business rather than as a stock trade, however, these fluctuations should be easier to ignore. One should be concerned with how well the business is run, opportunities for the business to expand, and the honesty and integrity of the CEO and various officers rather than how the stock price is doing on any given day or week. If the business grows and earnings rise, the share price will follow.

Because one will not have a large amount to invest early in life, shares will be bought over time, 100-200 at a time, until good sized positions are held (500-1000 shares) in a few companies. Maybe you'll have an interest in a growing internet company, a retailer, a restaurant chain, a healthcare company, and a software company in your portfolio after a few years of saving and investing. You'll be buying only the best prospects – there is no reason to select anything but your top pick in a sector. Unlike the mutual fund manager, you don't have enough money to affect the prices of these companies when you buy or sell, so you can concentrate as much as you desire.

The lack of diversification and the selection of younger growth companies will cause large gyrations in your account balance from month to month. Expect there to be months where your portfolio falls by 20% and others where it rises by 20%. While this would be foolish if you were only investing for a year, the long time horizon allows for you to be patient and wait for share prices to rise. While short term market forces may cause the price of some stocks to languish, eventually the growth of the business will lead to a growth in the price of the stock.

Hopefully you will pick a few winners (there will certainly also be some losers). As some of these winning positions become large (say, $50,000 or more), you would sell off some of the shares and use the proceeds to invest in other companies. The cardinal rule is again to never have more in one position that you would be willing to lose. This will lead to natural diversification as your portfolio grows.

As you grow older and have more capital to protect, some of the money would be put into more stable companies and placed into mutual funds. As discussed, this added diversification will help protect against events at any one company resulting in a large loss in your portfolio. A percentage of the portfolio would remain in your best-of-the-best picks, but this percentage would decline with time as you shift from asset growth to asset protection. This allows one to hold onto gains that have been made while still allowing for some growth.

Having outlined the life-long, serious investing strategy here, in the next chapter I'll describe it in more detail and provide a specific financial strategy linked to stage in life to become financially independent and ensure a comfortable retirement. I'll end this chapter, however, with a brief discussion of budget and spending choices that are critical to financial success. Before one ever starts investing, one needs to put his financial house in order. To start investing while deep in debt will only result in disaster. One will never be able to overcome the 18% rates charged by credit cards. Likewise, not having cash on hand to handle life's little calamities will result in needing to sell stocks and pay capital gain taxes and commissions each time a car breaks down or the furnace goes. Investing in individual stocks without putting away other funds for retirement is also not wise. Here are the things that must be done before you ever buy your first shares of stock:

1.   Save up an emergency fund of 3-6 months' worth of expenses. This will allow you to fix the car without needing to sell stocks or pull out the credit card.

2.   Pay off all credit cards and cut them up. Really. Start

paying extra on the smallest balance and then as each is paid, roll the extra money saved from not having payments into the next largest debt.

3. Pay off student loans and pay off or sell cars with large balances and buy less expensive ones for cash.

4. Fund your retirement accounts with 15% of your take-home pay in growth stock mutual funds in tax protected accounts. This will ensure you have funds for retirements even if you have terrible luck in stock picking.

5. If you have a home loan, refinance into a 15-year fixed rate loan. This will mean that your house will actually be paid off in 15 years, right around the time the kids will be looking at colleges.

Once you have accomplished the above, you are ready to start investing and growing wealth.

Chapter 5
The Investment Strategy

In this chapter I briefly lay out a money management strategy as a function of stage in life to allow you to build wealth. The next chapters then go into detail on investing in your early, middle, and late career stages. In the beginning less diversification is used since one has enough time to reduce the risk. In mid-life one begins to shift some assets to mutual funds and income producing assets since wealth preservation becomes more important. Late in life one is looking to live on one's income while having the portfolio grow with inflation to make sure the money will not run out. Let's now describe the stages in detail.

Stage 1– Early Career (Ages 16-30)

In the last chapter I discussed the three factors that affect stock market risk: diversification, volatility, and time frame. The typical investment advice will be to have vast amounts of diversification in order to reduce the risk posed by the volatility of individual stocks, but this does not take a young individual's time frame into account. The risk that the decline in the price of an individual stock or even the whole market will result in decreased return or even a loss can be reduced by holding stocks for long periods of time. An early-career individual, who has another source of income and 30 years or more to invest can tolerate the risk posed by less diversification.

Saving money for investing is the key during this stage of life. During this time one should be putting away money religiously because every dollar invested will be worth hundreds in 30-35 years. After you have put 10-15% away in a 401k, and saved $10,000 or so in a cash account for emergencies and handling life's little surprises, put away what you can in an investment account.

Unfortunately, this is also the time of life when one typically doesn't have much money to spare. While one won't have the financial burden of children in college yet, salaries are typically fairly low.

Many individuals will buy their own home in their late twenties after their career has gotten started. The mortgage is typically a substantial portion of one's income in the beginning. With time, the portion decreases as income grows with career advancement and inflation while the payment remains fixed, but the high initial amount of income consumed by a mortgage typically makes it difficult to find money to invest. (This is a neat feature of a fixed rate loan, that the burden becomes less with time. This is true as long as things are *left alone* and one does not decide to refinance the mortgage and take out money for kitchen upgrades every few years. Unfortunately, most people find the hard-won equity in their home just too tempting to leave alone. "Being normal" is being broke and never reaching financial freedom. Remember this when the temptation to "keep up with the Joneses" hits when your friend shows you her upgraded kitchen financed on a HELOC.)

Even though your income may be low, while young you should do your best to live below your income and save something each month, even if it is only a hundred dollars or so. Setting up automated processes, such as directing a portion of your paycheck into an investment account through direct deposit each month, can help those without the financial discipline to set money aside (which is most people). Saving also involves keeping expenses in check, however, since it makes no sense to direct money to investing while running up credit card bills. Below are some easy ways to save money for investing:

1)   Don't buy new cars. A quality used car that is 4-6 years old can be bought for cash for $4000-6000, will require far less maintenance than you think, last for at least 5-8 more years, and save you $4000 or more a year on interest and depreciation. Once you have $1 million you can buy a new car if you want, but you won't want to. Even then, buying 2 year-old cars is the best value.

2)   Minimize the amount spent on items that go down in value. Keep clothing, electronics, upholstered furniture, and other such purchases modest. For things that last (*e.g.* wood furniture) buy quality since it can always be resold. Also, buy second hand from estate sales to avoid the retail mark-up. Those antiques for sale will typically be of better quality than new items – after all, they've lasted a long time already.

3)   Never use credit cards. At a minimum, save up and pay cash for things, particularly decaying items. By paying cash, rather than putting clothes on credit cards, those clothes will cost a lot less in the long run. With interest rates at 15%-20%, you could easily be paying over 100% the cost of the item in interest if paying for things with credit cards and then paying them off in installments, which means you're paying double. Many people could easily put $300 or more away each month if they weren't paying credit card interest.

4)   Get water instead of soft drinks at restaurants. Ever notice that you order a drink, but only take a few sips during your meal? At $2 per drink, for people who eat out five times a week, that is $520 per person per year. Alcohol, at $5-$10 per drink is even worse. Order water – you'll barely miss the soda, save $1000-$2000 per family to invest each year, and save 150 calories per meal. You can buy alcohol at home for $1 or less per drink. (Note for kids: offer to give them $1 if they order water instead of a drink. They will probably do this 90% of the time. You'll save $1 per child, plus they'll learn that buying the drink costs money that they might rather spend on other things and probably be less likely to automatically order a drink when they are adults.)

5)   Turn to professionals. This may seem unintuitive, but if you have a big car repair, need to change a water heater out, or need to re-seed the lawn and you don't consider it a hobby, it may actually make sense to hire a professional to do it. If you are able to take on extra hours at work, that eight hours you would spend putting in that water heater (and really being away from your family, even though you're right there in the house, since they won't want to be around you with all the cursing going on) could be spent at work instead. If you pay the professional $200 and you get paid $30 per hour, you have just made an extra $40 by hiring the pro. Sure, by having the tools and experience *he* may only spend an hour doing the job, but if it would have taken *you* eight hours, what is the difference?

6)   Eat out less often. If you go out regularly, keep track of how much you are spending each month on restaurants. You may be surprised to learn that you are spending thousands of dollars each month. Try eating a few more meals at home each week. You can save about $50 per meal, or $2500 per year, just by eating one dinner in each week. If you get tired of TV dinners and frozen meals, pick up a copy of the *Betty Crocker* or *Better Homes and Gardens* cookbook and learn to make some simple dishes like pork chops or fried chicken. Another choice for busy people is to make crock pot meals – they're easy to make and ready when you get home. Give it a try – you'll be eating healthier and saving money.

7)   Avoid time shares. It may seem great to have that place waiting for you once a year, but you'll probably find that you're busy on that week or you just don't feel like going to the same spot year after year. If you simply rent a place when desired instead, you won't be paying all of those maintenance fees, have freedom to choose when and where you wish to go, and not have the headache of trying to unload a timeshare later. You will likely save thousands of dollars each year in maintenance fees and missed vacations.

Investing early in life allows more risk taking. Because you don't have a lot to invest, you should be more concerned with growth of capital than capital preservation in this investment account. A more detailed plan for investing at this stage in life is given in the next chapter. An outline of the plan is as follows:

1) Start buying large positions in the companies you feel should provide steady growth, once again evaluating the businesses when finding investments rather than focusing on stock price.

2) Once you've taken positions in a few stocks, add to these positions until you've bought as much as you would feel comfortable in losing. Once you have 500-1000 shares of your initial 2-3 choices, lock these in (forget about them) and start adding more companies.

3) Once you have built a position, reading through the annual report and glancing at the price once in a while is all that is needed. As long as the company has the same fundamentals for which it was purchased, the price really doesn't matter.

4) Once in a while (maybe every six months to a year) rebalance the portfolio. If you have a big winner, sell a bit and use the proceeds to buy shares in other stocks. In general, however, let your winners ride. As long as you don't sell your taxes and investment expenses will be low, allowing your gains to compound. If you are wrong some times, sell the losers, write them off against your winners (and up to $3000 of your regular income) and learn from your mistakes.

An alternative choice is to invest in mutual funds instead of individual stocks. This will reduce volatility, but limit your possible return to those of the market. Even still, investments should be concentrated in equities, probably starting by building up a position in a small cap fund, and then adding a large cap fund and an international fund as your balances grow. There is no reason to have a significant portion of your funds in bonds or income securities with so many years until retirement.

Stage 2– Late-Early Career (Ages 31-45)

By this point you should have seen your portfolio growing to the point that you have some real money in your accounts. If you have been a diligent saver, as defined by *The Millionaire Next Door*, you will have a net worth of at least:

Net Worth > (Your Age)x(Your Income)/10

For example, a 40 year-old with a $80,000 income would have a net worth of at least $320,000. You should have about $100,000 to $200,000 in a 401K, a paid-off or nearly paid-off home, and well funded college funds. In your taxable investment account you should have about 10-15 stocks and some fairly large positions in your portfolio ($20,000-$50,000). Hopefully you'll have a stock or two that has split several times so that your cost basis is almost $0 and the position is therefore almost all profit.

Somewhere in your early to mid 30's, when you have $50,000 or so in your investment account, you need to start looking at some capital preservation. You do this by shifting some of your money into mutual funds to get diversification, and some into smaller positions in the "income assets" described in Chapter 1. This would include large, mature stocks of companies that aren't growing rapidly but offer stability and predictability. These stocks will probably pay a decent dividend and grow maybe 5-10% per year, for a total return of maybe 10-15%. You will still have some large concentrated positions for growth (maybe 50-75% of your portfolio), but you also want to position yourself to hang on to what you have made.

Your 401k should also be in the hundreds of thousands by the time you reach the upper ages of this range. These funds will be in diversified mutual funds, giving you further diversification and protection. As previously said, since most people won't have a taxable stock portfolio or a well-funded 401k, you'll be better off than most of your coworkers even if you are a lousy stock picker and none of your positions in your taxable account do well. Note that you should still be putting 10-15% of your salary away into retirement accounts, not including any employer match.

Once again, you can also be funding an individual IRA with funds beyond the employer match, maxing out your IRA before returning to the 401k with remaining funding. If you have a spouse who does not work, you can also fund his/her personal IRA. This would be done before funding your own IRA.

Stage 3– Middle Career (Ages 46-58)

Here you should be in your prime earning years at work. You will probably have some significant expenses, like college, weddings, and more elaborate vacations. Hopefully you will have taken out a 15 year mortgage and have paid it off by this point. You also should become a millionaire during this time and wonder why you used to think a million dollars was a lot of money.

Despite your expenses, you should still have ample funds for investing, having paid off your house. You should be maxing out your 401k contributions and putting a large amount of money in your investment account each month. If your retirement accounts are sufficiently healthy, you may consider shifting a little more to your taxable account to generate income that is available to use before you retire.

Your investment account should be returning as much or more than your job. You will have attained financial independence, as described in Chapter 1. If you love your job, there is no reason to stop. If you don't, however, you will have the freedom to do whatever job you would like, so this would be a good time to look at a career change. Enjoy some of this money, but allow a majority of the income generated by your portfolio to reinvest in more assets and continue to grow.

Keep moving some of your funds into more diversified areas (mutual funds, quality stocks, bonds, REIT's, or maybe rental real estate). By the time you are 58 you should have at least 60% of your money well diversified, with the rest concentrated but still in amounts you can afford to lose, maybe $30,000-$60,000 amounts at the most. Remember also that the market can and does go down for periods of up to 10 years at a time, so you should have a year or two worth of savings in a nice, boring bank CD by the time you reach the end of this age range in case the market decides to crash and mess up your retirement.

Stage 4– Late Career (Ages 59-70)

Here you are finishing up your career, maybe working beyond 65 just because you want to. Hopefully you will have found something you love and never want to retire even though you could just give your salary to charity each month by this point. Your 401K and IRA accounts should have several million dollars in them, as should your investment account.

By this point most of your money should be well-diversified, including a number of mutual funds – some of which provide growth and others which provide income for expenses. Because you have so much money, you will also have a number of individual stocks, including some growth stocks and some larger, more stable companies that pay good dividends. You will also own bonds, REITs, convertibles, and other assets.

Note that if you started later, didn't put money away, or don't have the large accounts listed for some other reason but are in this age range, you should only have the very diversified portfolio of mutual funds (no single stocks) because you'll need to make sure you preserve your assets. You should also be working hard and saving all you can. The clock is ticking.

Stage 5– Retirement/Second Career(Ages 70+)

If you started investing in your early twenties or thirties and have been following the advice of this book, you should have gained financial independence at about age 45. At that point you should have had enough money in investments to replace the income from your job - somewhere between $750,000 and $1.5 million dollars. From that point your portfolio should have continued to grow (since you kept your job, or at least found another that you really liked, and therefore didn't withdraw much of the interest from the investments). Hopefully though you did take some of the money to improve your house, take some nice vacations, and otherwise lived life a bit. Even with a little lifestyle mixed in, you should have between $10 million and $50 million by now, making you one of the elite decamillionaires.

At this point, since you'll be living off of your savings, you'll need to be generating income and selling assets as needed. A good rule-of-thumb is that you can take about 4% each year from an account without the balance declining over the long-term. You can take 8-10% if you don't mind seeing the balance decline. For example, if you do have $15 million and would rather spend some of it than leave it to your heirs.

Because you cannot tolerate risk as well as you could when you were working, you must keep a portion of the portfolio well diversified. Set this portion of the portfolio up so that you receive enough income to not need to sell shares very often (although if taxes on interest are high compared to capital gains, it may be better to sell a few shares here and there to gain living expense money). Good choices are blue chip stocks, REITs, investment real estate, utility stocks, and drug companies. (More will be said about setting up an income portfolio in Chapter 8.) Make sure you have spread funds out to guard against devastating events, like fraud, bank collapses, etc…, because these are the only risk you really will be facing.

If you have substantially more than you need to generate income, you can continue to have a portion of your portfolio in concentrated stock positions. This is because you can afford to take risks with money you don't need for living expenses. You can also have a greater portion of your money in stocks than the recommended amounts since you can withstand a large market decline without affecting your standard of living. Because of this, your rate of return will be substantially better than that of others who save just enough for retirement.

If you have less assets than you would like, such that you are barely meeting expenses withdrawing 4% of the portfolio each year, you should still have the diversified portfolio to preserve what you have. Unfortunately you've lost the luxury of time, which reduces the risk of being more concentrated. You should also have sufficient liquid assets (in a savings account) to pay for expenses for at least 5 years since you won't be able to sit through market downturns. You'll need to use proceeds from your portfolio for living expenses regardless of market conditions.

Having briefly covered the investment strategy and how it relates to each stage in life, the following chapters provide more detail on money management and investing for different stages of life. Getting it right when you're young is probably more important than anything you do in mid or late life. Ironically, this is when people make the most mistakes, and there are all sorts of temptations to get on the wrong path. It is very tempting to borrow to get the lifestyle you want quickly rather than wait until you have the financial resources to pay cash. This is especially difficult given that everyone around you is doing so. Chapter six therefore includes a lot of detail on budgeting and lifestyle management in addition to information on starting to invest.

Chapter 6
Early Life Investing

Probably the most critical time for determining your financial future is between the ages of 16 and 30. The most important thing is to establish the money management practices that will enable you to save and invest. This is really not that hard – it all comes down to not going into debt and spending less than you earn – but most people do a poor job of it because they want "everything now." Unfortunately, this is the culture in which we live and everyone around you will be living beyond their means. This is why there are so few millionaires even though it is within many people's grasp.

In this chapter, I therefore begin by discussing how to get your finances in order so you're ready to invest. A section on budgeting and finding ways to save money for investing follows. After that how to set up an investing plan is discussed, followed by how to set up investment accounts and buying your first stocks. Finally, some common investing strategies, like dollar cost averaging, round out the chapter.

Setup Your Cash Flow to Grow Wealth

Cash management for growing wealthy is really quite simple. While most people make sufficient income from their jobs to grow wealthy, few do. The reason is very similar to the reason that many people struggle with weight loss – one must consistently do the things that make you wealthy while everyone around you is doing the opposite. In fact, while most people know that restricting calories and getting exercise is needed to maintain a healthy weight, few people understand what it takes to become wealthy. People with a wealth-building cash flow are therefore very rare, hence the small number of millionaires.

The main reason is that most people don't have cash flow left for saving and investing is that they grow their obligations each month (the house, cars, watercraft, credit cards, vacation homes, club memberships) until all of their income is spent before they see it. To grow wealthy, a portion of income needs to be placed in assets each month. One needs to free up cash to go to investments, either by increasing income or limiting liabilities. Obviously increasing income is the less painful approach, but for most people the key is to reduce liabilities since they have more control over liabilities than income.

Gaining money for investing requires setting up your family cash flow in such a way that you have money to invest from each paycheck. You then allow funds to build until a suitable sum is amassed, and then buy assets (individual stocks or shares in a mutual fund). These assets, in turn, generate more income that can be be reinvested to buy even more assets.

With the typical consumer household, interest payments and liabilities grow with time. Interest owed then increases debt, which generates more interest owed. In contrast, families who become wealthy have assets which generate interest, which in turn is reinvested to create more interest. Rather than debt working against them and consuming earnings, interest works in their favor to help them build wealth. The four steps to create a wealth-building cash flow are therefore to:

1. Minimize recurring payments.
2. Eliminate debt (especially credit card debt).
3. Set up automated paycheck withdrawals to investment accounts, or having the discipline to write a check each month.
4. Acquire assets

We'll now say more about each of these steps.

1. Minimize recurring payments

It is difficult to find money to invest if most of your money is obligated to recurring payments before the month begins. To break the cycle, look at what bills you have every month and see which can be eliminated. Can you get rid of a car payment and pay cash for a good used car from a private owner? Do you really need that health club membership? Could you jog in the park? Can you eat in more often? Do you really need the Netflix subscription or an expanded cable package? Could you use a less expensive phone plan? Most of all, can you get rid of various consumer loans and stop paying interest payments?

Any bill that you can eliminate will mean that much more money can go into investing. See what things you can go without. If you have a lot of automated monthly charges and subscriptions, particularly for things you don't use regularly, see if you can cancel some things instead and just purchase the goods and services as you need them. You may find you spend a lot less when you actually buy things when wanted.

Probably the easiest way to prevent having all of your money spoken for before the month begins is to keep your lifestyle in check when you start working. Set aside 10% of your paycheck and put it into a mutual fund each month so that you will never get used to having that money to spend. If you get a raise, put half of the raise in the fund to easily increase your savings. If you get "found money" in the form of a tax refund or other windfall, invest it rather than following the typical urge to spend it.

2. Eliminate debt

When you have debt, not only are you buying a lot of things you can't afford, you are paying more than their cost when you do so. If you buy something on a credit card and pay the minimums, you will pay many times the value of the thing you bought before you pay it off.

It takes will power to save up for things, and sometimes it seems like you really need them now and there is no other way but to use debt. But if you take going into debt out of the equation, you'll find all kinds of creative ways to get by until you save up the money. Also, if you pay cash rather than pulling out the credit cards, the next time you need something it will be that much easier to afford since you'll have more cash available if you are not paying off debt and you can save your whole paycheck.

3. Set up automated withdrawals
Investing regularly is the secret to doing well in the stock market. If you invest the same amount each month, when the market is low you will buy more shares. When the market is high you will buy less. And because the natural direction of the market over long periods of time is up, you will do well if you stick to a plan. One of the easiest ways to do this is to set up automated transfers from a bank account to an investment account. Many people will find it difficult to send a check every month, but will find that if the money is withdrawn automatically, they will tend to leave things alone and do a better job of investing consistently.

4. Acquire Assets
As stated in Chapter 1, assets are things that grow in value over time and generally provide a source of income, either through their sale or because they pay dividends or interest. Initially, the additional income from assets may not amount to much. For example, purchasing $2000 worth of stock, earning an average of 10% a year, would only provide $200 in income the first year. But if stock were purchased on a regular basis, such that $2000 per year was purchased, in ten years that would provide an income of $2000 per year. Furthermore, if

the proceeds from the stock were used to buy more stock — reinvested — compounding takes over and income really grows fast.

Eventually, income from assets will exceed income from employment, at which point one becomes financially Independent. Because income grows as the value of assets grows, the rate of growth accelerates with much more money being earned in later years than in initial years.

For example, at 10% interest rate with compounding, meaning that the income generated is reinvested, assets will double every 7 years. So in 7, 14, 21, 28, 35, and 42 years, a $1000 initial investment will be worth $2000, $4000, $8000, $16,000, $32,000, and $64,000, respectively. Multiply this value by 10 or 20, to account for a $10,000 or $20,000 investment instead of only a $1000 investment, and you can see why you never want to take money out of a retirement account. It may seem like taking out that $10,000 to upgrade your home makes sense when you're 30, but it will be worth $6.4 million when you are 72 if you let it grow.

Note that $32 was made for each original dollar invested during the last seven years. Income starts small, but grows enormous with time. It is important to invest early and then to wait to make withdrawals as long as you can.

So while it may not seem like much initially, start accumulating assets even if it is only a little at a time. With time, some of the income generated by assets can be used to supplement employment income, but once assets are purchased, never spend the original capital. It is amazing how quickly wealth can grow with persistence.

Finding Money for Investing

Minimizing expenses and putting money away for investing sounds great, but how is it actually done? Often it seems like it is impossible to find money to put away, especially when you are just starting out in a career and there are all sorts of expenses. Some suggestions for reducing expenses and freeing up cash flow were given in Chapter 5, but without careful control impulse buys will eat away at the money you save. Creating a budget where income and expenses are listed, allocating income to the necessities first, and then purposefully reducing optional expenses until the needed cash flow for investing is available is the only sure-fire way to make sure money will be available each month for investing. In this section we'll look at how to use a budget to allocate available funds and generate money for investing.

Budgeting and planning are just math and mechanics that anyone can do, but actually following the plan requires discipline and motivation. This is where will power and determination will decide whether you reach you investment goals or fall short and be like everybody else. This is similar to following an exercise plan. There will always be a little voice inside of you trying to keep you on the couch (and plenty of "friends" giving you every excuse in the book not to take that run). Things will also always come up that will make you want to deviate from the plan. Here are some tricks to help keep you on track:

Actually develop a budget on paper: Most people think they can just control their spending without budgeting. People fear being constrained in their spending, even if it is just a sheet of paper with some numbers on it. They also don't want the hassle of tracking their income and expenses.

Using a weight loss analogy again, most people will also think that they can lose weight without counting calories. The trouble is that without looking into how many calories are actually in the foods you are eating, you may have what you think is a little snack or just a few sodas and really be doubling the number of calories you are eating in a day. Sometimes it is not the entree but the sides that are adding all of the calories.

Most of the trouble in finding money to save and invest isn't the big items like the home mortgage. It is the regular latte after work or the snacks bought at the convenience store. It is going out for dinner because you don't feel like cooking and the junk you are buying at Wal-Mart that you didn't plan to buy. The fact is, most people who start budgeting actually start to feel more wealthy because they find all of the money that is getting sucked away that they don't even know they are spending.

Execute the budget: Now that you have the budget, the trick is actually executing it. Here again, this is where many people fall short. Obviously, your recurring expenses are what they are and one will not go over budget there. The issues are things like food, clothing, household, and yard maintenance items that end up costing more than you expect.

Realize that retail stores are designed to get you to buy things you were not intending to get. You walk into the supermarket and see a great sale on laundry soap and buy some even though you weren't planning to buy soap this week. The hardware store has a display of tools and you find yourself picking up a set of screwdrivers even though you have a set at home and have no intention of using them this month. You're walking through a department store and see a display of shirts or socks or something and think, "Hey, I could use that." Next thing you know, you have blown your budget. This is what you were trying to avoid in setting up a budget.

One way to avoid going over budget is to use a cash and envelope system. Beyond ensuring that you can't accidentally spend more than intended for a category, using cash will actually cause you to spend less since people tend to spend less with cash than they do with credit. In this system you bring home cash at the start of the month, or perhaps every two weeks, and place it in envelopes corresponding to the expenses for which it is meant. For example, you could have a clothing envelope, a food envelope, and a home supply envelope. You then only buy items corresponding to the category on the envelope and when you are out of cash in the envelope, you stop buying items in that category.

This may take some iteration at first since you may find food costs more than you think, even if you are careful in what you buy. If this happens, you need to return to the budget (with your spouse, if you are married), figure out where the money will come from, and adjust the budget. While it may seem silly at first, this type of discipline will stop you from making spur-of-the-moment decisions that will blow the budget. After a few months you should have a good handle of how much money is needed for each of the different categories.

Can you go without an envelope system? Yes, but you need to be willing to track what your costs are by saving your receipts and subtracting what you have spent from your total for the category as you go. It is probably easier to just use envelopes and cash.

Find spare cash to increase the free cash flow in your budget: If you have developed your budget and discovered that you don't have any cash left over, or it is such a small amount that it won't really matter, you'll need to find ways to increase your free income. Obviously this is done by either finding ways to make more money or by finding ways to cut back on spending. Over time your income should grow naturally if you can advance in your job, so it may be a matter of making sure your spending doesn't increase with your salary (perhaps by setting aside half of each raise you receive, as discussed previously). There are also temporary things you can do to raise your income, perhaps to pay off a loan that will eliminate a payment and free up some cash. You can work overtime for a while if you have that option, find ways to make money on the side, or even take a second job delivering pizzas or working as a cashier. There is also usually temporary work available during the holidays. Really, if you can generate an extra $1000 per month for a few months, you might be able to pay off some credit card bills and thereby increase your cash flow. You should remember, however, that these are temporary fixes and can't be done indefinitely.

There is also the spending side of the ledger to consider. One huge source of spending is meals out. One can eat for a couple of dollars per meal at home starting from scratch, which does not even cover the tip in a restaurant. If you can learn to cook, you can save a lot of money, eat healthier, and enjoy meal time with family.

Don't have time? Consider making a large pot of something and eating portions during the week and freezing portions for future weeks. If nothing else, when you do cook, cook one extra portion and take it to work – you'll be the envy of your office. Also do time savers like making one big salad you can use for several days and having tomatoes, cucumbers, and other fruits and vegetables that don't hold up well on the side. You can do the same thing with a soup or a pot of beans.

Other places to consider cutting back are hobbies (maybe take up kite flying or hiking instead of golf), snacks (consider having a six pack of Cokes in the office fridge rather than buying one from the vending machine each day), and subscriptions (do you really need to be in the Cheese of the

Month Club?). Finally, if you own something that costs a lot of money for upkeep (like a boat or a condo), it would probably be better to just rent one when desired instead of continuing to own unless you use it almost every weekend. You'll probably find there are others things you'd like to do besides being down at the dock cleaning the boat all the time.

Now that we've covered the strategy of using a portion of your income for the acquisition of assets, and using a budget to find cash to invest, we're ready to look at putting the pieces together by developing and executing an investment plan. Specifically, the next section provides details on developing an investment plan where the money saved through budgeting is first used to create a wealthy person's cash flow. Then, the steps to actually start executing the plan, including how to enter the stock market, are discussed.

Setting Up an Investment Plan

Everyone has seen the late night advertisements. There is a guy standing in a large backyard by a sky-blue pool with tropical flowers and a large house in the background. Perhaps he has a woman 10-20 years younger than him lounging next to him in a bikini, enjoying the sunny day. They are both probably wearing sun glasses – wealthy people are always wearing sunglasses. He says that he is ready to share the secrets to building great wealth and obtaining economic freedom.

He then proceeds to tell you that you can make a fortune while you keep your day job using his system. It may be a real estate trading scheme. You may be buying and selling penny stocks. Perhaps you are doing multi-level marketing — a technique only a hair different from a pyramid scheme. Maybe you are selling products over the internet for them. All you need to do is set up an account and then check each day to see how much cash you made. Just sign up for their seminar, which conveniently is coming to the Holiday Inn near you. The price is never mentioned.

Unfortunately, wealth will not come to you from some scheme. If there really were a scheme that could create untold wealth, why would they share it with you? Why not just sell the real estate themselves? Why wouldn't they set up their own websites to sell their products? If the individuals in the commercials actually are wealthy (and they didn't just rent out a house for the infomercial), you can bet that they got that way off of the fees for their seminars and classes, not from the scheme they are presenting.

Real wealth doesn't come from a scheme or luck. There is no special secret. Everything can be calculated. It comes from a plan. A good investment plan involves selecting investments based on time available, taking appropriate risks, and doing things consistently. Let's look at each of these aspects:

1.   Time. Growing wealthy requires time, so a good investment plan involves starting to save and invest early in life. As stated before, with compounding very little interest is made in the first few periods, but huge amounts are made during the last few. Try this experiment: Start by placing a penny in a jar. The next day place two pennies, the next day four pennies, and so on, doubling the amount each day. See how much you will be putting in the jar by the end of thirty days.

2.   Risk. Growing wealth requires that risks be taken, because risk is correlated to reward. This does not mean going to Vegas and betting on red. It means investing your money in places where the odds are in your favor, but that grow faster than the rate of inflation. Things like stocks, real estate, ETFs, mutual funds, and bonds. These investments allow your money to earn money and compound, growing as you work so that eventually your portfolio is providing more income than your job. This is when things really start to happen.

3.   Consistency.   Discipline is required in a good investment plan. Money needs to be put away every month into investments. It doesn't matter if the market is up or down, put some money away. If the market falls through the floor, buy all you can. If the market seems really pricey, perhaps hold back a bit on the side in a money market account, but put some in anyway in case you are wrong. No matter what, save some money each month from you earnings. Consistency is the key.

The first two aspects work together, in that by having more time available, greater risks can be taken. The third aspect, consistency, is needed to avoid trying to time the market and thereby sabotaging your investments by missing the big gains. Remember that plans are done ahead of time when things are calm and thought can be given. One should be reluctant to change a plan, particularly in emotional times.

In setting up the plan, time and risk are used to determine the types and allocations of investments. As available time for investing grows, risk should as well. If you are investing for 30 years, you should heavily favor quality growth stocks. For 5-10 year investments, some high dividend, established stocks and bonds should be worked into the mix. Of course, one's risk tolerance (as determined by one's stomach for oscillations) is also involved in the decision. With these aspects in mind, we now turn to the specifics of setting up the plan.

1. Develop a cash flow plan. The first step in an investment plan is to develop a cash flow plan. A cash flow plan includes the basic elements of a budget, in which income from work is balanced against expenses to plan how money will be spent or saved.   A budget, however, only balances spending and income.   A cash flow plan goes further, showing how a portion of income is diverted to the purchase of assets, which in turn then produce additional income streams.   It shows how funds flow from wages, to one's bank account, and out to expenses and investments.   Income from investments is then shown flowing back into the bank account, as occurs when assets are purchased.   It is the purposeful direction of this cash flow where income is directed to buy assets, which in turn are used to produce additional income, forming a circular cash flow path that leads to growing wealth.

Developing a cash flow plan is the first step to ensure a reasonable amount of your income is going towards investments.   It is in this plan that you look at your income and expenses and pare back on expenses until you have some money left for investing.   In particular, you want to direct some of your income to required investing (paying for retirement and college for your children) and your optional investing (that which builds assets that will give you additional income in your forties and beyond) before it gets obligated to other things.   The steps for building a cash flow plan are as follows:

a) Start by listing all of your yearly income from work at the top of a sheet of paper.   Find the total and write this below the income sources.   Form a box around this area and label it "Income."

b) Below the income box, in the middle of the page, draw an empty box and label it "Cash-On-Hand."

c) Next, on the lower left side of the sheet below the cash-on-hand box, list your obligated expenses.   Include things like rent or mortgage payments, insurance, utilities, and car payments and other legal obligations.   This is money that you are legally obligated to spend or it damages your credit, puts you in jail, puts you on the street, or leaves you in the dark. Draw a box around these, total them at the bottom, and label the box "Obligated Expenses."

d) In the bottom middle, below the cash-on-hand box, list your necessities like food, gasoline, and clothing. Estimate a yearly amount for these items and total it at the bottom. Draw a box around these and label it "Necessary Expenses."

e) On the bottom right side, below the cash-on-hand box, list luxuries. These are things you could do without but like to do, like hobbies, kid's activities, eating out, and vacations. Make an estimate for each of these and write a total at the bottom. Box these in and label it "Optional Expenses."

f) On the left side of the page, next to the cash on hand box, list required saving accounts such as retirement accounts (401k's and IRA's) and college savings accounts. Allocate 10-15% of your income for retirement savings and fund college accounts at least $2,000 per year per child. Label this box "Required Investing."

g) Finally, draw a box to the right of the cash-on-hand box and label it "Saving and Investing." Place a line for an emergency fund account and one for an investing account.

At the bottom of the page, create lines for the totals of the income box, the expenses boxes, and the investing boxes. In the end your income will match the sum of the expenses and the investing. Note that all of the money needs to go somewhere because otherwise it will be wasted. There can be no slush funds.

Draw an arrow from your income to the cash-on-hand box. Draw one from the cash-on-hand box to each of the expenses boxes and to each of the investment boxes. Draw an arrow from the saving and investing box back to the cash-on-hand box. This shows how money will flow from you income to cash-on-hand (when you bring home the check), then to either expenses or investments.

Note that your savings and investments also generate income which comes back to your cash-on-hand, which is represented by the arrow from savings and investments back to the cash-on-hand box. This is the difference between the cash flow diagram of a person who will grow wealthy and one who will be average. The average person will not have this income from assets adding to their cash-on-hand. Instead the average person will only have income from work. The number of obligated expenses will also be larger, including interest on debt, so income will simply flow into cash-on-hand and flow right out again into expenses. There may or may not be required investments to fund things like college and retirement. His income may increase and he may be able to buy nicer luxuries, but he will always be dependent on his job to meet all of his needs – a tenuous position.

At the bottom of your cash flow diagram, subtract the total of your obligated expenses, necessary expenses, and required investing from your income. This is your free cash flow – money that you are free to obligate to optional spending or investing as you wish. Figure out which of your optional expenses are most desirable, fund those, then allocate a reasonable amount based on your free cash flow to saving and investing (at least $200-$300 per month if you can). Divide the remainder of free cash flow to optional spending and saving and investing as desired until the sum of your saving/investing and expenses matches your income.

If you don't have enough money for saving and investing, look at your optional expenses and see what can be trimmed. Also see if your necessary expenses can be trimmed at all (for example, finding ways to save a bit on food like eating out less and making a few less expensive meals each month). Perhaps you can carpool to save on gasoline and set the thermostat down a little to save on utilities. Early in life when your income is low you should expect to be scrimping and saving. This is the time to just enjoy living simply rather than the time to be buying all sorts of things and taking lavish vacations. That comes later.

At this point in your life don't expect anything to come back from your investments (that arrow from the saving and investing box that points to the cash-on-hand box). Any small amounts of income that your investments do generate should be reinvested to grow more assets. With time, however, you will start to receive enough income from your assets to allow you to increase your optional spending. If you need motivation, plug your savings rate and a reasonable estimate for rate of return – 12-15% is appropriate – into an online interest rate calculator and see how much your investment portfolio will be worth in 10, 20, and 30 years. You'll be amazed.

The income and expenses portion of your cash flow diagram then becomes the start for your yearly budget. From there, create monthly budgets to handle the variance in expenses and, perhaps, income throughout the year. Use your cash flow diagram as a guide and ensure you are keeping expenses at or below the yearly limits and directing money as needed into investments to meet your plan. The growth in your portfolio value will not be steady, but it will happen if you consistently save and invest. Most of the increases will happen within a period of a few months over several years.

Each year, revisit your cash flow diagram. Add new expenses as needed and remove those that end. Adjust the income as appropriate and keep your retirement investing at 10-15% of your income. As your income grows, increase your saving and investing by a reasonable percentage while also increasing your optional expenses. It is fine to enjoy life more as your income grows, but keep directing some of the increase to saving and investing before it is fully consumed by other things. Remember that income invested can be spent over and over again, rather than just once.

2.   Allocate your investments to different assets. The second step in developing an investment plan is to allocate the money you have available for investing to different types of assets. This includes both determining how much will go into each type of asset (stocks, bonds, real estate, etc...), and whether individual stocks and bonds or mutual funds will be purchased. These decisions are based on personal tolerance for risk.

As discussed previously, concentrating investments mostly in growth stocks will cause account balances to fluctuate rapidly, but will provide better returns over long periods of time. Adding a small percentage of bonds will help smooth out the turbulence but will cause a reduction in returns. Money invested in mutual funds will add diversification, which will also tend to reduce the level of price swings and provide more reliable returns, but investing in single stocks will allow the possibility of making returns substantially better than the market.

You should decide what percentage of investments to allocate to each type of asset. Being young, you should favor growth over income, stocks over bonds, and return over preservation. Still, you should consider how you would feel if you saw a sudden drop in the value of your portfolio. If you would hold pat or even buy more, you are able to tolerate the fluctuations that high levels of equities and single stocks provides. If not, mix in more bonds and stick mainly to mutual funds.

3. Begin to implement the plan. Once an asset allocation plan is developed, it is time to start purchasing the securities. This will be done a little at a time as sufficient cash in your investment account is available. For example, if the plan is to use mutual funds and you have raised $5000 in cash – the minimum needed by the mutual fund company – you might go ahead and purchase the first fund. If the plan is to have 80% stocks and 20% bonds, you might then put the next $5000 into the same stock fund, then put the next $5000 into a bond fund. More money would then be added to the stock fund until the desired 80%/20% ratio was achieved.

At some point you might raise an additional $5000 and buy into another stock fund in a different asset class. For example, if you started in a large cap fund, you might buy shares next in a small cap fund. Gradually, by adding money to each of the funds as available, you will build a portfolio with the planned investment mix.

The same thing can be done with individual stocks and bonds. Here a first stock is selected once one has enough funds to buy a reasonable number of shares – normally 100 shares. Additional shares of various stocks and bonds are then purchased as funds are available. In this case it is good to have a watch list of about 5-10 stocks. As funds are available, 100 shares of the stock that is at the best relative price would be purchased.

Once the desired asset mix is attained, it should be loosely maintained by purchasing the necessary funds or individual stocks and bonds as needed to keep the planned ratios. Some amount of rebalancing should also be done if the ratios get too out of spec by selling some funds/securities and putting the money into others. This should be kept to a minimum, however, since doing so will likely result in capital gains on which taxes must be paid, and also result in commissions and other costs. Rebalancing should be done at most once per year.

Setting Up A Brokerage Account and Start to Buy Individual Securities

In the previous sections the development of a cash flow plan and an asset allocation plan, collectively known as an investment plan, were discussed. In this section we cover the mechanics behind setting up a brokerage account and starting to invest in stocks (as well as bonds and other assets). Only the investment in individual stocks is discussed, although investing in Exchange Traded Funds (ETFs) is done the same way. Mutual fund investing is as simple as finding a fund family online and setting up an electronic deposit or sending in a check. Vanguard is a great fund family for low cost funds – the kind you want.

The stock market offers a rare chance to make a greater return than savings accounts and outpace inflation. Most people do not know how to take that first step, however, never having had a family member who was an investor. Investing really isn't as difficult as you think, but there are some logistics required. One also needs to change one's mindset from expecting regular, predictable returns from a savings account to expecting more sporadic but higher returns from investing.

To start investing, begin with the following steps:

Step 1 – Set up a brokerage account. There are many online and in person/by phone brokers available. Those without a lot of financial experience would probably be better off with a full service broker (for example, Merrill Lynch) because they will give more guidance and help with trades. If you go this route, find a broker who is willing to teach you as you go rather than one who will simply recommend investments without telling you why. The latter is often more interested in selling you products and making money for the firm than helping you do the best job investing.

A discount broker will give great service and know how to enter trades, but will expect the client to select their own stock picks. There are several of these that can be found online or in advertisements in newspapers and financial magazines. When selecting a discount broker, finding one that offers low commission prices and provides the other account services you want should be the goal. For example, some investment accounts provide a debit card that allows you to easily access your account. Others may sweep any cash in the account into a money market fund automatically.

Step 2 – Select a list of stocks to purchase. The next step is to develop a list of buy candidates and begin following them, waiting for a good moment to enter the market. Ideally these stocks should be in different industries. For example, a restaurant chain, a retail business, a bank, a railroad, and a technology company. Try to find the best pick in several different markets.

There are various services that provide information on stocks. An excellent source of stock reviews is the *Value Line Investment Survey.* The subscription price is fairly high, but most libraries have a subscription that can be used for free. I believe that any subscription should pay for itself with increased investment returns, and Value Line will do that if you invest regularly. Start with the list of stocks that are rated 1 for Timeliness (Near the back of the index) and then find those that have a safety of at least 3. From there, review the full-page descriptions of companies of interest (the page number is listed in the index), read about what they do and look at earnings growth, debt levels, and other factors.

Step 3 – Begin to follow the stocks of interest. Follow the prices and watch the price graphs on Yahoo finance or another site. Get a feel for how these stocks will behave. Perhaps even create a fake account of $10,000 and pretend to buy shares of some of the companies. Then, track the value of the portfolio for a period of time.

Once you feel comfortable that you know what to expect in the way of price movements, you'll be ready to make your first real purchase. Look for one of the stocks on your watch list that seems to be in a good spot to buy based on its price history (for example, it is a bit off of recent highs).

Step 4 – Buy 100 shares of your top pick. Even if you have a lot of money to invest, wade in gingerly. Start by purchasing 100 shares and watching the shares for a while. This allows you to buy more shares on dips (which helps psychologically) and get a feel for how you react with real money on the line.

Step 5 – Buy 100-200 more shares of your top pick on the next dip in price. It is unlikely that you will catch the best price on the first try. Instead, plan for the stock to decline a little and pick up some more shares when it does. This allows you to bring down your average purchase price (called your "cost basis"), and also puts you ahead of the game when the stock moves up to the price you paid for the original shares, instead of only putting you even.

Step 6 – Find your second pick and buy 100 shares. Follow the same pattern as described for your top pick. Continue to acquire shares until you have 200-300 shares in the second company. Do this again with a third company, and perhaps a fourth and fifth company.

Step 7 – *Grow your positions.* By the time you have bought shares of four or five companies, you probably have exhausted your watch list. As you raise more money to invest, pick a good entry point in one of the companies and buy more shares. Continue this until you have 500-1000 shares, or as much as you would be willing to lose in any one position, whatever that level is based on your personal situation and risk tolerance.

This process is continued as you gain more money to invest. If any of your positions grow so large that you can't stand the loss (because stocks do decline rapidly) sell a few shares and invest in another company or add to your other positions. Eventually you should have 5-10 positions and a portfolio worth $50,000-$100,000 (this may take several years if you are working and adding money to invest as you go) if you have a high tolerance for risk. If you have a weaker tolerance, spread it out to 15-20 stocks.

If this still seems too risky and you're always worried about losing money, setup a portfolio of index mutual funds instead (as covered in Chapter 10). You may not have the right mindset for buying individual stocks and will always be worried by the fluctuations and latest news stories about the stock market. There is no shame in buying mutual funds instead of individual stocks, and you will still make inflation-beating returns. Many advisers say investors are foolish to buy individual stocks at all and that most people will do better just buying index funds. There is certainly a lot of evidence to support that position. We'll discuss the choice between common stocks and mutual funds later in the next section.

Note that in saving up money and investing each time you have enough cash, you are doing what is called *dollar cost averaging* automatically. In dollar cost averaging, one invests a fixed amount of money on a regular basis. For example, an investor may put $1000 in a mutual fund every month regardless of market conditions or other factors.

By fixing the amount, the effect is to buy more shares when the price is relatively low, and less shares when the price is relatively high. In doing so, even if the market stays essentially flat – just moving up and down between a couple of limits – because more shares are bought at the lower prices the cost basis will be below the average of the price range, so a profit will be made. This is a very automated, easy, no-decision way of investing that is a good approach. It can also be improved upon, however.

Looking at the chart for any stock, one sees that the price tends to increase for periods, then decrease for periods. For a company that is growing (the kind recommended here), the long-term lows will always be higher than the previous lows, and the highs higher than the previous highs. This is called an "uptrend". Because the stock does not move randomly, as it falls in price it becomes more and more likely that it will stop falling and move upwards again (again, we're talking about stocks that over the long-term are growing). The modification to the dollar cost averaging strategy is then to wait for periods where the stock has fallen in price before making investments. In doing so, a better price will be gained than that gained through blind averaging.

Choosing when to buy with this method is somewhat arbitrary. One could buy when the price falls for three days in a row, or when the price drops by 10% or so. Obviously a method should be chosen such that the stock can be bought regularly. Waiting for the price to drop by 20%, say, before making a purchase, may result in few shares actually being purchased while the stock climbs to the sky, leaving you behind.

Stocks Versus Mutual Funds

Before leaving this section on starting to invest, I thought I'd say a word about the choice of buying individual stocks or mutual funds. As discussed in Chapter 2, stocks provide a unique niche in that the growth rate for stocks is above that of inflation, and yet the risk involved is not so substantial. Buying single stocks carries special risk, however. While the stock market in general tends to go up over time, individual companies do not always do so. There are very few companies around today that were there fifty years ago – some are bought out by other companies, but others lose out to competition or other factors and disappear.

While there is a possibility that the whole amount invested may be lost when investing in single stocks, the likelihood is fairly low. Maybe one in twenty companies will go bankrupt and stop trading in a three to five year period of time. Still, if you buy single stocks regularly, you will eventually have a few that go under.

Even if the company that one buys does not disappear, the stocks of many companies sit where they are for many years, even if the economy in general is expanding. If you were to buy a single stock and wait, your rate of return could be much worse than that of the market in general.

The likelihood of a total loss declines to approximately zero if several stocks are bought rather than just one or two. As was previously discussed, this process, called diversification, also causes the amount of volatility to decline since stocks that go down are balanced by stocks that go up. Because the economy in general is normally growing, the balance on the account will normally grow with time (10-20 years) and at a rate higher than inflation, typically by 5-10%.

For this reason, diversification is used to reduce the risk presented by single stocks. The difficulty in investing with small amounts is that there is not enough money to buy positions in several companies directly. To gain substantial diversification in individual stocks would require $50,000-$100,000.

To allow diversification without having a lot of money, many people choose to invest in mutual funds, which pool money from groups of investors to buy a portfolio of stocks. Most mutual fund companies have minimum initial investments in the $1000 to $5000. Some will also allow investors to invest less provided that they sign up for automated purchase such that a fixed amount is invested each month.

The need for large amounts of diversification right from the beginning, however, is questionable. If you have the right mindset and are willing to "roll with the punches" for the opportunity at a higher return, starting with individual stocks may be a good choice. When you are just starting and you do not have a lot of money to invest, the amount that could be lost in any one individual stock is fairly modest and can be replaced fairly quickly if you are saving and investing regularly. For example, if an individual only has $2000 to invest, while the entire amount could be lost if invested in a single stock, the $2000 loss could be easily regained through work. In addition, the risk due to concentration in a few positions is muted by long-term investing and careful stock picking. There are many who say that an investor must be extremely lucky to be able to beat the market, but then again there are a lot of investors who do through long-term investment in great companies.

Perhaps the biggest reason to choose mutual funds over individual stocks is how one reacts to market volatility. With individual stocks one should expect greater volatility. It is not uncommon to see stocks rise by 100% or more in a year or fall by 50% or more. If this type of roller coaster ride makes you worry and keeps you from sleeping at night, investing in a mutual fund where the large amount of diversification will reduce the levels of the fluctuations might be the right choice. If you can stomach the ups and downs and stay calm, however, individual stocks may be the way to start.

In actuality, there is really no reason to choose either individual stocks or mutual funds. While an investor may start out investing primarily in individual stocks, as a portfolio grows some funds should be shifted to mutual funds for quick and easy diversification. Likewise, one starting in mutual funds should shift a small percentage of assets to individual stocks once the portfolio grows large enough to allow for additional, targeted gains. A longer discussion on mutual fund investing, including tips on setting up a mutual fund portfolio, is given in Chapter 10.

Chapter 7
Mid-Life Investing

In the last chapter the strategies for money management and investing for those just starting their careers was discussed. Hopefully the reader found this book when he was at that stage of life and is already leading a fiscal life far different from his peers. If not, there is still time to improve your financial situation, but it will take a little more sacrifice.

At this point the book shifts to the strategies that an individual at mid-life would employ. This is loosely defined as the time between maybe 35 and 50. As you enter this age range, in your career you're starting to enter in your greatest earning years. Expenses for things like home maintenance and children's activities are also starting to grow. I start by discussing changes to investment style and then move into a discussion of fiscal management suitable for this stage of life.

Beginning to Diversify

When an individual begins to enter the middle phase of his working life, asset protection begins to become more important. To recap, early in his career the individual seeking to be financially independent would be living on less than he made and putting money away regularly for investing. Because he had relatively little to invest, he had little to lose. This, combined with a long time horizon that allowed for recovery from mistakes and just plain-old bad luck meant that he could be aggressive with his stock investment.

Remember also we're only talking about investments beyond traditional retirement plans. He would also be putting money away regularly in his work's 401K plan and perhaps a personal IRA on the side. The IRA might also have some individual stock holdings, but the 401k should be entirely in mutual funds, as should a portion of the IRA. This would ensure that even if his individual stock investments didn't work out, he would still have a retirement equivalent to his peers. Actually, better than most since many of his peers would not contribute to their 401K's and IRAs or cash them out at some point in their lives once the balance started building up.

Being aggressive did not mean being foolish. He would still invest in a way that would put the odds in his favor. This included investing for the long-term where growth in a stock's price could be expected to follow the growth in intrinsic value of the stock he was buying. Likewise, he would be buying shares only in companies with steady earnings growth, good management, and room for continued business growth. He wouldn't be trying to time the market or playing various investing "games" since he knew that the odds in those games were stacked against him.

The risk he would be taking was concentrating his holdings in a few great stocks rather than spreading his money out over dozens of stocks or buying an index or mutual fund and just accepting market returns. He would be concentrating his investments in a few companies that he believed would outperform their peers over the long-term. Because bad things happen to even good companies – officers steal money or cook the books, new regulations are created that hamper the business, competition emerges that takes a large amount of the company's market share, or they drill a hole in the bottom of the ocean and kill everything in the area – he would be taking the risk that one of his selections could decline substantially in value. He would know that the price of the shares of any individual company can decrease rapidly or even become worthless in a short amount of time and take that risk into account.

However, while the entire market does not increase in value that rapidly, averaging about 10% per year, it is not that uncommon for individual stocks to double or even quadruple in the period of a year. If one is fairly good at picking stocks, one can therefore make up for one or two bad stocks that go nowhere or even disappear with one great stock that goes up twenty-fold over a period of 10-20 years. In the early stages, our young investor is trying to find one of these stocks to make his meager holding grow rapidly.

After several years of investing for growth and growing in his career, he should reach a point where he does start to have enough money to begin to protect it. In his personal investment account, he may have 6 to 10 large positions worth about $10,000-$15,000 each, with an account balance of fifty to one hundred thousand dollars. (Note, he should also have a like amount in a 401k, which would be invested in an array of mutual funds.) At that point, he should start diversifying his holdings to reduce risk. As stated before, diversification reduces risk because holding a basket of stocks or other investments reduces the damage done by the collapse of any one asset. Even if a company doesn't fail outright, the advances by some stocks in the portfolio will offset the losses or stagnation in other stocks.

The amount of risk reduction afforded by diversification depends on two factors: 1) The number of different positions held, up to a limit of about 50-100 stocks, at which point further diversification has little effect, and 2) the amount of covariance among the holdings.

To achieve a larger number of positions, the easiest method is to take a portion of the portfolio and put it into mutual funds. Because their costs are lower and they perform as well as managed funds, index funds are a good choice.

121

The covariance is a factor that determines how much different assets you hold tend to move in the same direction. Two holdings with a covariance of one would move in lock-step. This would mean that investing in these two holdings would offer no more diversification than putting all of your money in just one of them. An example of two assets with a covariance near one would be an S&P500 fund offered by American Funds and another offered by Vanguard. Except for differences in fees, these two funds should move in concert with each other.

Likewise, the price movements of two investments with a covariance of zero would have no relationship. An example here might be investments in the housing market in France and Washington DC. While it is possible some global event might affect both markets, in general the changes in price between the two investments would be fully uncorrelated.

Finally, two investments with a covariance of -1.0 would move in exactly opposite directions, where one would go down 10% if the other went up 10%. An example of would be a call option and a put option on the same stock at the same strike price. Because the call option would become more valuable if the underlying stock went up, while the put option would be come less valuable, they would move almost directly opposite to each other. Note that covariance is a mathematical way to express the correlation between assets that was described in Chapter 4.

Ideally, the covariance should be about zero among the various holdings in a well diversified portfolio. To achieve a portfolio of assets with low covariance, buy funds in different asset categories. For example, buy a large cap fund, a small cap fund, a bond fund, an international stock fund, and a real estate fund (REIT). One could also toss in a commodities fund in small amounts if inflation was a concern. Buy some funds that pay a large dividend (ideally hold these in an IRA to protect yourself from taxes) and buy others that pay almost no dividend but hold a large number of growth stocks. You can also select managed funds that try to buy based on value (an example would be a "Dogs of the Dow" fund) and another that invests based on momentum.

Shifting to Income Investments for Stability

In addition to diversification, the types of assets held will begin to shift as you age and gain wealth. This shift will start slowly in mid-life and then accelerate as you approach retirement age. During the initial years of investing the focus should be on growth, and stocks with good growth potential should be selected. As one accumulates assets, however, the focus should shift towards preservation of funds by changing the types of assets which are held, if ever so gradually. This is done in part by shifting a portion of one's portfolio into income assets that help provide preservation of wealth. In Chapter 1 we briefly discussed income assets. A more thorough treatment is now given.

While corporations are not people, they have a life cycle similar to people. There are the initial years when they are fiscally weak and maladies that a more mature company would weather with ease might wipe them out. They then have the growth years when they are expanding, going into new regions, adding new products, and perhaps buying out competitors. At some point they reach a state where they are nearly fully mature and start to grow a lot less (at least in terms of percentages – it is a lot easier for a company making $1 million per year to double revenues than one making $1 billion dollars per year).

As discussed in Chapter 1, companies that are either late in their growth cycle or entering their mature phase are stronger financially than their younger brethren. Their prospects for price appreciation are less because it is difficult for large companies to increase their earnings substantially in percentage terms. Still, they are able to withstand downturns in the economy and challenges by competitors fairly easily. These companies also are likely to pay a sizable portion of their profits out as dividends since they need less money to grow the company.

While these are not the kind of stocks that will go up 1000% percent over the next several years, the chances of them disappearing completely are relatively low (although it does happen eventually for every company). In addition, the payment of a dividend means that the investor will receive some income even if the economy, and therefore the market, is fairly flat. As previously discussed, the dividend will also protect the investor somewhat from decreases in price since as the price drops the yield of the company will increase (assuming the dollar amount of the dividend remains the same), making shares of the company more desirable.

In mid-career one begins to worry less about growth of wealth and more about stability, so the stocks of companies that still provide some growth but which are less susceptible to market downturns and certainly less likely to go bankrupt are sought. The kind of stocks that provide stability are older, larger companies that pay a good dividend. Other suitable assets are REITs, which have a good interest payout due to the rents collected on properties owned by the trust, and corporate bonds. Limited partnerships are also a possibility, but you must be careful since buying into one may greatly complicate your taxes.

Because income assets described tend to pay a larger dividend or interest rate than young growth stocks, the investor will be generating income each year on which taxes must be paid.

This will greatly reduce your return over the period of several years. In addition, the tax rate will be at the highest levels since the income will be on top of your income from working. It is therefore wise to place as many of these types of assets as possible in your IRA or Roth IRA, where they will be tax deferred or tax-free, and then keep mainly growth stocks that don't pay a dividend in your taxable trading account.

Changing Financial Goals at Mid-Life

In addition to changing your investment strategy because your investing goals change, as you transition from early life to mid-life your money management strategy shifts since your financial goals begin to change. In your twenties you're probably worried about landing a good job and choosing a career path. Buying a house and starting a family are also probably on your mind. You financial goals should be things like getting an emergency fund together, working your way into a reliable used car that will allow you to go several years without a car payment while having reliable transportation, starting an investment account and starting to buy a few stocks or mutual funds, and starting a 401k and an IRA and funding both as much as possible.

As stated near the start of this chapter, by mid-life you should have accumulated a fair amount of wealth if you started in your twenties. You'll have somewhere between $100,000 and $250,000 in your retirement savings (401K and IRA). You should also have maybe $50,000 to $100,000 in your investment accounts.

If you bought a home with a fifteen year loan and haven't taken out any equity, you should be paying the loan off and have $100.000-$300,000 built up in equity in your home. This is assuming a salary of between $50,000 and maybe $80,000 per year. If you are making $150,000 or more during that time because of your profession or location, you may have home equity of a half million dollars or more.

This puts your net worth somewhere between $250,000 and $650,000. For comparison, in his book, *The Millionaire Mind*, Stanley defines individuals who are prodigious savers (those who are likely to become wealthy in their lifetimes) as those who have a net worth of their income times their age divided by 10. For someone making $60,000 who is 40 years old, someone who has at least $240,000 would fit this profile. Having a net worth of around half a million dollars puts you in a very select group of individuals – those who are very likely to become multi-millionaires on middle class incomes.

The financial goals for someone in middle age should be the following:

1. **Paying off your home.** Hopefully when you bought your home you got a 15-year fixed loan with a payment of less than 25% of your take-home pay at the time you took out the loan. By the middle of this age range you should therefore be close to paying off the loan even if you were only making the standard payments. With raises at work, your income should have increased to the point where making extra payments should be easy. With kids going to college, it would be nice to have an extra $1000 per month to put towards books and tuition. You might even consider paying cash for a small house for your children at the college rather than paying money to rent them an apartment, building up equity in it while they go to school, and the selling it or renting it out when they graduate. With your children there to keep an eye on the property, it would likely be safe to rent one or two of the rooms out to other students to help generate more income from the property while your children are in school.

2.   **Shoring up your retirement savings.** If you have not been saving and investing as religiously as you should have been, now is the time to do everything you can to make sure you have enough money to carry you through your retirement years. You will need to have, at a minimum, $200,000 for each $10,000 worth of income you will need to replace. It would be better to have $300,000 - $400,000 for each $10,000 of income needed since withdrawing at that rate increases your chances of not reducing your assets.

To increase your income, look for overtime, and think about selling things or services on the side. To cut your expenses, think about things you can cut or liabilities you can sell to allow you to save more. There will come a time when you are not able to work, and having enough savings will make all the difference in your quality of life.

3.   **Starting to enjoy life more.** If you have done a good job of saving and investing, including putting plenty away for retirement, you should start to enjoy the fruits of your labor. You can start to take some of the vacations others around you were taking with credit cards in their twenties, except you can pay cash. In this way you saved on the interest so you are able to buy more things than your coworkers after doing the same amount of work. You get the other advantage of not coming home to an onerous credit card bill.

You could look at buying a beach house or a cabin in the woods, putting in a pool or a hot tub, or maybe finishing a basement or an attic to add a game room or a movie room. This all starts through budgeting, where you allocate some of your investment income each year to supplement your income from working.

Chapter 8
Late-Life Investing

Having built up assets during your early years, seen those assets compound and really grow, you are starting to get to the point where you're ready to start using your investments as your primary source of income. If you've done a good job of saving and investing, you should have more than enough for a comfortable retirement. In this chapter we discuss how to begin to transition from gaining income from a job and using investment income as a supplement to setting things up for retirement income.

We'll start by talking about transitioning your finances to be ready for living in retirement and transitioning your portfolio to reduce volatility, a process started near the end of the mid-life period. We'll then go into rolling over retirement accounts and starting to gather income from them. We'll then talk about investing strategies specifically for generating income and making assets last. Finally, we'll touch on the topic of planning to give some assets away to heirs and charities.

Getting Ready For Retirement

Once you enter your mid to late fifties, it is time to start transitioning your finances to get prepared for living on a retirement income. This means paying off any outstanding loans that remain and cutting expenses where possible. You need to start thinking about how much money you'll need your assets to generate and make sure your savings are large enough.

At this point it is a good idea to estimate your monthly expenses and determine how much you'll need for basic costs. A standard rule-of-thumb is to expect your retirement expenses to be about 80% of your working salary, although those with high income jobs like executives tend to spend a lower percentage of their pre-retirement salary in retirement. This is because there is no longer a need to spend money on expensive clothes, dry cleaning, and meals out due to a lack of time.

It is therefore better to estimate what your expenses will be, starting from a list with estimates for each item, and then roll them up into a total. Realize also that while work related expenses such as business clothes and gasoline may decline, medical expenses will likely increase as many seniors are on a regimen of medications. Also look at the cost of hobbies, travel, and activities you plan to take part in once you retire and have more time. Consider including a couple of low-cost or free hobbies, like playing cards with friends and hiking in the park – instead of choosing all high-cost hobbies like golf and home renovations.

Once you've determined an estimate for retirement expenses, sum the values and find a yearly total. Then turn to your assets to estimate how much you can generate in retirement income. A good rule-of thumb to prevent exhausting one's funds is to not spend more than about 5% of the value of a portfolio during any given year (a 3% spending rate would be more conservative). Assuming you plan to spend up to 5% of the value of the portfolio each year, your savings should be about 20 times the needed yearly income in retirement. For a $50,000 per year income, this would require a million dollars in assets.

To understand this withdrawal rate, assume that the portfolio will grow at about 10-12% each year (the historical growth rate for equities). As long as no more than 5% of the portfolio is withdrawn during any given year, the return of the portfolio should be enough to provide sufficient income and make up for losses due to inflation. Of course, if you can build up more assets before retirement, such that you can limit the amount you take out to 3% per year or less, you decrease the chances of your savings not lasting through your retirement even more.

One consideration, particularly if your retirement savings are somewhat lacking, is to sell your home and downsize into a town home or apartment-sized condo. This will allow you to add some of the equity from your home to your savings. It will also reduce the amount of maintenance you'll need to do on the property and allow you to reduce the amount of furniture and items you have. This is a great time to distribute some family heirlooms and other items to your children. This will keep them from fighting over items after your death and is the best way to ensure your things are distributed according to your wishes. You may also discover that none of your children want one of your cherished pieces of furniture or collectibles, leaving you free to sell the item for additional retirement spending or to give it to someone who would cherish it as much as you.

Transitioning from Growth to Income

In retirement, the goals are to 1) preserve funds so that they last through the remainder of your life and 2) generate current income for living expenses. This is done by shifting some funds to lower return but lower risk assets that pay regular income payments and to diversify holdings. This means shifting from growth assets like small company stocks and into bonds and dividend paying stocks.

Generally one is told to shift funds into bonds gradually to increase stability and reduce risk as one gets older. As previously stated, there is an old rule of thumb for allocating funds between stocks and bonds often credited to Jeffery Bogle, founder of Vanguard. It says that one should hold a percentage of stocks equal to 100 minus his age, and the rest in bonds (or equivalently, hold a percentage of bonds equal to his age and the rest in stocks).   For example, an individual who was 40 years old would have 40% invested in bonds and 60% in stocks.

Note that the term, "stocks," really refers to more volatile, growth type investments.   This would include smaller companies that pay little or no dividend and tend to have a high beta (large fluctuations), but that can be expected to have relatively high returns if held for a long period of time.   The term "bonds" refers to more stable investments that tend to pay a good dividend or interest payment, and would include high quality corporate bonds; treasury bonds; preferred stocks; common stock in mature, stable companies; and REIT's.

The idea behind holding one's age in bonds is that when one is young and can afford to take risks, more money should be in investment vehicles that offer the potential for higher returns. This is both because the younger investor can better suffer a loss and because the he/she has time for his/her investments to mature. As the investor ages and can less afford to take risks– and when more current income is needed from the investment account – money is shifted into investment vehicles that should not be affected as much by market events. These investments primarily provide return through dividends and interest so that the holder can still receive income during downturns.

During the stock market fall 2008, I heard several people say that they had planned to retire, but now would continue working because their 401k balances had fallen so far. Because the bond funds held up reasonably well even though the stock market was down around 50%, if these people had been following the rule, they would have only lost about 20% (65 years = 35% stocks, 50%*35% = 18% loss). They could have therefore gone on and retired since they would have been able to live on income from their bond funds while waiting for the stock portion of their portfolio to recover. In fact, when they rebalanced the account, they would have sold some bonds and bought more stocks (to regain the correct percentages of stocks and bonds) and actually done really well in the recovery that ensued.

While it is a good idea to shift some funds into income producing assets as one gets older, the rule-of-thumb to own your age in bonds was created when individuals weren't living or working as long. It should therefore be adjusted if one is planning to work longer. In addition, there is a case to be made that one should not hold many income-producing assets when one is a decade or more away from retirement in any case since stocks have always increased in value over periods of ten years or more. Still, income assets will provide gains even when the market is stagnant, so holding some income assets can be an advantage during some time periods.

Taking Control of Your 401K

Many people who leave a job also leave their 401k account with their old employer. While theoretically the money is safe, at least from shenanigans from your former employer, the investment choices you had in that 401k plan were not necessarily the best. It is therefore wise to take the money with you.

The same goes if you are retiring. While it may seem easier to just leave the money, it is best to take control of it yourself so that you'll be able to cut the fees you pay (with a 401K, you pay administrative fees on top of the fees charged by the mutual fund company) and have the money readily available for when you need to take required distributions and perform other such actions.

About the worst possible thing you can do is to have the HR

department simply write you a check. You will then have a portion of the funds withheld for taxes and need to file for a refund the following Spring to have the money returned even if you do deposit the remaining funds into an IRA. Worse still, if you deposit the check into your savings account instead of depositing them into an IRA, you will owe taxes on the entire balance of the 401k that year, which can be substantial if you have a lot of money left in the account. Handled properly, you can allow the money to grow for many more years before taxes are taken out of it. If you have not yet reached retirement age and don't roll the funds into an IRA, you might also need to pay huge penalties. In the end, you will see about half of your money disappear to taxes and fees.

The correct thing to do is to do a direct roll-over to an existing or new IRA account of the same type as the 401k (standard or Roth). In this the funds are directly deposited into your IRA account from the 401k without ever being in your possession. Doing so will prevent any money from being withheld, requiring you to file to have the money refunded at tax time. Once in the IRA you can invest the funds as you see fit. Note, as I remind the reader constantly in this book, taxes can get tricky (and the rules can change from year to year), so it is well worth the money to consult with a CPA before making any movements of the money from your 401k. Doing things the wrong way can be a very expensive mistake.

Unrolling an IRA

Hopefully you will have saved up enough money and cut expenses enough in preparation for retirement to not need to touch your IRA for the first several years. So long as it is in the IRA, it continues to grow tax deferred (or tax free, if it is a Roth IRA). Unfortunately, the government is itching to get their hands on those dollars, so they will eventually force you to start withdrawing money. For a traditional IRA, the age at which you must start taking withdrawals is currently 70 and ½. The amount of the withdrawals is based on the average life expectancy – basically withdrawal rates are such that all of the money will be withdrawn by the time you pass away.

There is a strategy in making withdrawals from an IRA. Ideally in the early years you will have enough dividend and interest paying assets in the account to produce enough cash each year to cover the withdrawals. This means that you can just let the cash from dividends and interest build up, withdraw this cash at the end of the year, and then let the process start again. This will work for a while, but the required amount of the withdrawals will increase each year (the government wants it all out by the time you reach the average life expectancy) so eventually you'll need to start selling assets and pulling the proceeds out.

When doing so, start by selling things that are just not doing well and don't have the promise they once had. For example, if you bought a stock but the business you expected never materialized and the stock has been flat, you might as well sell it rather than sell shares in a company that is doing well. Likewise, if you have a stock that has had a good run but now has reached a plateau and the growth rate has slowed considerably, you might as well sell it. Since the tax paid will be based on the amount withdrawn regardless of how well you did on the investment, it doesn't matter whether you are taking a loss or not.

It is also a good idea to try to keep dividend and interest paying assets in the IRA as long as possible. Because you will pay taxes each year on the interest and dividends when you hold income stocks and bonds outside of the IRA account, while you will only pay taxes on the capital gains when you sell an equity that has appreciated in price, it makes sense to keep the income producing assets sheltered as long as you can.

I would therefore sell a growth stock on which I'd had a capital gain, withdraw the funds from the IRA, pay the taxes and then reinvest in the stock again if I wanted to continue to own it before I would do the same thing with a stock I was holding for the dividend or a bond.

Managing Investments in Retirement

Once you have actually retired and started living on income from your assets, you'll need to manage your withdrawals and investments to protect your wealth and maintain your lifestyle. There are actually three things that funds must be protected against in retirement. The first is that the portfolio might be exhausted through spending before the end of one's life. The second is that the value of the portfolio may drop due to market fluctuations. The third is that inflation wastes away the value of the portfolio, forcing one to lower one's standard of living.

Prevention of running out of money is done by making reasonable withdrawals for living expenses based on the value of the portfolio. (Note this requires you have a big enough portfolio to cover living expenses, which means you need to start planning and investing when you still have many years to build up your assets.) Typically a withdrawal rate of 4-5% of the portfolio value each year is small enough to almost ensure the money will last. Some strategies start lower and increase withdrawals to keep pace with inflation.

The larger your portfolio, and the lower your expenses, the more risk you can take with the money and therefore the greater return you can generate. For example, if you have $5 million in assets and need $80,000 per year in income, you could probably use $2 million to generate enough cash for expenses and then invest the other $3 million in stocks for a higher return. As the stock portfolio grows, you can divert some of the profits into your income generating account and increase your income. On-the-other-hand, if you only had $2 million in your portfolio and needed $80,000 per year in income, investing a significant amount in equities would be too risky.

Protecting oneself against drops in portfolio value is done by holding enough wealth in cash (money market funds and CDs) to pay for near-term expenses, and diversification for money not needed immediately. Holding cash ensures that one will have the money needed to pay for expenses no matter what the market does over periods of a few years. After most market declines, previous price levels are regained after a period of one to five years. For this reason having enough money in cash instruments to last five years is typically enough. Ten years almost guarantees the ability to weather a storm. Money can be invested in CDs of staggered terms to maximize returns, *e.g.*, money not needed for three years would be in a 3-year CD, while money needed next year would be in a 1-year CD and so on.

Money not needed within the next 5-10 years must be invested to prevent loss to inflation. These funds should therefore be invested in common stocks, bonds, and real estate (either directly or through REITs). To reduce the risk of loss and reduce volatility, investments should be well diversified – spread over several different mutual funds, types of assets, and areas of the market. The goal here is not to beat the market but instead to simply make returns greater than inflation while reducing the chances of loss of capital as much as possible. Ideally during major stock market declines the bond and real estate holdings will limit losses to 10-20%.

Given this basic strategy, we now turn to different strategies for structuring a portfolio to provide the needed income, inflation protection, and principle protection. We'll start with

137

the traditional strategy of buying income producing assets to provide the needed income. We'll then turn to alternative strategies of generating income through capital gains or option writing which is appropriate when interest rates are too low to generate needed income from income assets.

Creating an Income Portfolio

The goal of investing in a traditional retirement portfolio is to generate enough income to pay for expenses so the principle can be left intact. There must also be a growth aspect to the account to both preserve the account value and keep the purchasing power of income generated constant despite the ravages inflation. Ideally one would like enough cash to be generated from income and dividends to meet monthly expenses such that the sale of securities would not be needed. When interest rates are sufficiently high this can be accomplished easily using bonds, high yielding stocks, and perhaps real estate assets.

The typical retirement investments — those that pay a good dividend — are:

1. Utilities – Because utilities are typically not in a growth phase, but instead simply collecting money from rate payers and distributing the profits to shareholders, utilities typically pay good dividends.

2. REITs - Real Estate Investment Trusts hold a portfolio of real estate, typically concentrated in a certain type. For example, there are REITs that focus on office buildings, apartment buildings, shopping malls, and even cell phone towers. These generally generate good income from rents that are passed along to shareholders.

3. Limited Partnerships – These trade like stocks and are typically tied to some income-producing source such as a big steel ore pit or a set of oil distribution pipelines. Much of the income received is passed to the partners.

4. Preferred shares – These are special shares of stock that a company issues when it wants to raise money for some purpose. They typically pay a large dividend and can have special features like the ability to convert to common shares at some ratio.

5. Bonds – These are loans made to companies and pay interest twice per year and at some point in the future return the principal to the lender (the bond holder). If interest rates do spike because inflation picks up, as it did in the 1970's, one could be set for retirement by buying into bonds paying very high rates and then holding onto them as interest rates subside. Bonds are currently paying too low a rate right now, however, due to the low-interest rates on government securities, to be worth the investment.

Another option that would require a little more work is to buy rental properties that generate rental income. This is not always the best option since it either requires one to become a landlord/repair man or hire a manager who will take a substantial amount of the profit, but it is a way to create an income when the interest rates paid by traditional income investments is low or for those who just enjoy owning real estate.

To set up an income generating portfolio, simply diversify among the different options listed above. Rather than having income that is generated be reinvested, as was done when you were younger and didn't need the cash for expenses, simply have the cash go into a brokerage money market account or be direct deposited into a bank money market account. You'll want to have a little cash cushion in this account – perhaps a year's worth of expenses – to avoid being short on cash when an expense is due.

If you are investing through mutual funds, things are fairly simple. For example, you could put 25% each in a total bond fund, an income fund (which would invest in both bonds and stocks), an REIT fund, and maybe a hybrid such as a convertibles fund (which would buy convertible preferred stocks and bonds). These should generate income throughout the year that would be deposited in your money market account.

If you are investing in individual securities, you'll need to structure things yourself to ensure you'll be receiving income payments as needed throughout the year. Bonds typically pay interest payments every six months, so you may want to buy some bonds that pay in January and June, and then some others that pay in April and September, for example. Most stocks pay a dividend four times a year. Some also pay a large dividend at the end of the year, which is useful for things like home property tax payments. Limited partnerships often provide a small payment throughout the year like a dividend and then provide a large payment at the end of the year, as do REITs.

One final consideration is saving on taxes. If you have the ability to generate more income than you need, you'll want to avoid paying taxes on income that you reinvest if you can legally do so. As stated previously, one way to do this is to keep assets that generate excess income in your IRA or 401k accounts and then keep most of the equities you own in your taxable accounts. Because the equities only generate taxes when you sell them, you won't need to pay taxes on gains on them so long as you leave them alone to grow.

The assets that generate income needed during the current year can be in a retirement account or in a taxable account since you'll be paying the same taxes on the income either way if you take and use the money. As with a 401k, you are required to withdraw a certain amount each year, as determined by your age after you reach 70 ½ years old. If this is the case, you'll want your retirement account to generate at least as much cash as needed for the required distributions each year to avoid selling assets if possible.

Generating Retirement Income When Interest Rates Are Low and Fixed-Income Assets are Overpriced

Generating enough income to pay for expenses in retirement is a fairly simple thing (provided that account is large enough) when interest rates are reasonably high and bonds and dividend paying stock prices are consequently low. One can just select a set of dividend paying stocks such as utilities, buy a few bonds, and then collect the dividend and interest checks. If the income from these investments is large enough one will never needed to sell stocks to raise cash or touch most of the holdings at all.

When interest rates on quality corporate bonds are in the 8-10% range and stocks are paying 5-8% dividends, one can easily generate $50,000 per year on dividends and interest with a million dollar account. Many people – foolishly, I believe – even invest their entire retirement savings in bank CDs when interest rates are high enough. This may be "safe," provided they don't live long enough for inflation to zap their savings, but they are not getting anything near the income they could have gotten without a lot more risk. They are also steadily losing a couple of percentage points to inflation every year. This is true if CD rates are at 0.25% or 25% because they will always pay less than the rate of inflation. Really you're paying the bank a little bit each year to hold onto your money for you!

Unfortunately there are times like the current period where interest rates are too low to generate enough income to make the traditional strategy work. This is usually because the Federal Reserve has lowered interest rates to near zero, as they currently did due to our real-estate bubble bursting, or as the Japanese did in the 1980's when their real estate bubble burst. Unfortunately, we're currently having about the same sort of luck the Japanese did, so interest rates may stay low for a long time.

Having low rates means more than just needing to accept a low rate of interest. When rates are lowered, the price of income producing assets go up as investors go from safe bank CDs into more risky assets like corporate bonds and dividend stocks in an attempt to get more income. When rates eventually rise again, either because of an action by the Federal Reserve or because inflation starts to pick up, the price of these assets will fall. Someone buying these assets at high prices will both not get the interest rates he should and be taking a risk of losing capital when prices reset to more normal levels.

When interest rates are low, one must be more creative to earn a return from a portfolio. Some options are:

1. Continue to hold a set of index funds and sell some shares periodically to raise cash. This unfortunately requires selling stocks and is subject to market fluctuations, but by keeping enough cash-on-hand to cover expenses for a five to ten year period, risk can be cut substantially.

2. Write covered call options to generate income from stock holdings. This requires more effort than other strategies since positions must be resent every couple of months, but has the advantage of being able to cause any stock to generate an income. There are also some management companies that will perform this function for the investor. Note one must be

142

careful to maintain sufficient diversification while employing this strategy. You generally need to buy a lot of shares (at least 500-1000) in a single company for call writing to be profitable. This can be risky if this causes you to have only a few large positions.

Let's look at each of those options in detail.

1. Generating Income through Capital Gains

The first method to generate income during low interest rate times is to hold equities for capital gains instead and simply sell some of the equities each year to generate the needed income. Over long periods of time equities will generally return between 8% and 15% per year, so one can comfortably sell between 3-4% of assets each year, withdraw the money from the portfolio, and still maintain the account balance while keeping inflation at bay. As stated previously, a reasonable amount of cash investments should be held to reduce risk, say 5-10 years' worth of expenses, so that one can suspend withdrawals during years like 2008 where the market declines considerably rather than needing to sell right after a major decline when stock prices are unreasonably low.

The sale of a fixed percentage of the portfolio each year is easy and straightforward, but is not necessarily ideal. Remember that the market is like a river with deep sections, rapids, and eddies. You know that you will eventually get downstream but the speed at which you do so will vary. Sometimes you'll even go back upstream a bit. Because you can't see downstream – just where you are and upstream – you don't know if you are about to shoot down a rapid or spin back upstream in a whirl pool. You do know, however, whether you just made a lot of progress or not, and you know that on average you'll make about 8%.

A strategy that takes advantage of this knowledge, rather than blindly selling a fixed percentage of the portfolio each year, would be to time when you sell assets and raise cash based on conditions in the market. When you've had a good year, you sell some assets. On bad years, you hold pat and let your assets recover. The cash position that you hold affords you the ability to delay sales on bad years since you can use some of the cash position to pay for expenses when the market does not perform well.

This strategy might work as follows:

a. Start out with a cash position of 7 years' worth of expenses.
b. At the end of the year (note that most stock market gains will occur between October and January), if the portfolio gained more than 15%, sell enough assets to raise two years' worth of cash.
c. If the portfolio gained more than 10%, sell enough to raise one year's worth of expenses.
d. If the portfolio gained less than 10%, leave the portfolio untouched and spend the cash instead.
e. If the cash position ever drops below five years' worth of expenses, sell enough assets to regain five years' worth of cash.
f. If the cash position ever equals ten years' worth of expenses, don't sell no matter what the portfolio value did.

In this strategy, assuming that 4% of the portfolio was to be spent each year, on years when the portfolio gains at least 15%, you would sell 8% (two years' worth of expenses). On years when it gained 10-15%, you would sell 4%. On other years you would leave the account alone. This means you would be selling shares after rallies, when stock prices were high, and holding after modest gains or declines.
At times where there are a string of bad years, such that your

cash drops below 5 years' worth of cash – the minimum that is fairly safe – you would bite the bullet and sell some shares. If there are a string of good years and you've gathered a large cash hoard, you would keep the extra money invested so that you don't hold cash for a long time and lose money to inflation.

2. Writing Call Options to Generate Income

A second way to generate income when dividends are low is to use options in a strategy known as *covered call writing*. This is definitely a strategy worth knowing and is fairly low risk, but I have had mixed results. Here I'll present some background, discuss the risks, the provide an example and some lessons I've learned in practice. Note that options were covered briefly back in Chapters 2 and 3 and the call option was introduced at that time. The reader is encouraged to go back and review these sections if needed.

Covered Call Writing – Some Background

Covered call writing is a way to create a flow of income even if a stock does not pay a dividend, reduce risk, and even do better than investing for capital gains in flat markets. In writing a covered call, an investor who owns shares of a stock (the *call writer)* writes a legal contract to another individual (the *call buyer*) which gives the second individual the option (but not the obligation) to buy the shares for a predetermined price. In exchange for the right to buy the shares, the buyer pays the writer a fixed amount called a *premium*. Just like a coupon, the offer is only good for a limited amount of time and expires on a specified date. After that date, the contract is null and void and the option writer is free to hold onto the shares or write and sell another contract. The writer also keeps the premium.

To simplify the pairing of option writers and option buyers, an

145

exchange – the Chicago Board Option Exchange (CBOE) – was created. The CBOE set up standard expiration dates and creates an "orderly market," which means that there are regulations on how option buyers and writers are brought together and standardization in the terms of the contracts. For example, all options for a month expire on a specified Friday (actually Saturday morning, but trading stops after Friday night) each month. This arrangement with the CBOE also frees the option writer from needing to actually write a contract. Writing an option is as simple as calling your broker or pressing a few buttons online.

There are specified intervals for the selling price, called the "strike price." In general strike prices are set at $5 increments, except for lower priced stocks that can be set at $2.50 increments. The expiration month for options can be written for several months out (about 6 months). As discussed in Chapter 2, there are also longer term options called LEAPS that can last for several years.

In writing an option, an investor calls his broker with the name of the stock, the expiration month, and the strike price. For example, a holder of 1000 shares of Apple might contact a broker with an order to write 10 Apple July $100 calls (a call option is the right to purchase shares at a specified price, a put option is the right to sell shares at a specified price). This would give the buyer the right to purchase the 1000 shares of Apple at any time between today and the expiration date in July for $100 per share. Note that each call gives the right to buy 100 shares. In exchange for this, the writer might collect $200 per call, or $2000 total.

The price received, called the *premium*, is based on three factors. 1) the price of the stock, 2) the time until expiration, and 3) the level of volatility in the price of the stock. Let's go through each of those factors:

1) The price of the stock.

The first factor affecting the price of options is the price of the stock on which the option was written. Obviously, if Apple stock was trading at $110 the day the July $100 call option was written, the buyer would be willing to pay at least $1000 per option, since he could exercise the option, pay $10,000 per 100 shares, and turn around and sell the shares for $11,000. If the price of the stock is above the strike price, the option is said to be "in-the-money" and will sell for the difference between the share price and the strike price plus a little more.

An option below the strike price will still have a value (due to the other two factors to be described). Such an option is said to be "out-of-the-money." Obviously, an "out-of-the-money" option is less likely to be worth anything before it expires (like having a coupon to buy shoes for $100 each when they are on sale for $90), and therefore the premium collected from their sale will be less than that for in-the-money calls.

2) The time until expiration.

Options that are good for a long time are worth more than those about to expire. Going back to our example of a coupon that gave you the right to buy a pair of shoes for a certain price, a coupon that gave you the right to buy shoes at $100 per pair for three years would be worth more than one that expires in a month, particularly if shoes are currently selling for $90 per pair but they might sell for more in the future. (This is actually the main reason options were invented – to allow people who need a product in the future, like wheat, to lock in a price rather than take a chance of not being able to afford the item later.)

In general the amount of the price of an option that is due to the time until expiration stays about constant until about 90 days out, then begins to decay rapidly. This means that when writing calls it is worth it to sell calls that expire 2-3 months out because you'll get a lot more per call than if you sell one that expires in 20 days, but it is not worth it to sell them for 6-months out because you won't get that much more for the extra three months and you run a greater risk of the stock price ending above the strike price or the shares falling in price before the expiration.

3) The volatility of the stock price.

The volatility of the stock price also affects the price of the options since a stock that moves quickly with large fluctuations in price is more likely to close above the strike price than one that does not. In our shoe example, if the price of shoes is going between $90 and $120 per pair from week-to-week, your coupon that allows you to buy them at $100 would be worth more since that might be a bargain when you wanted to actually buy the shoes. If shoes had sold for around $90 per pair for years with little change, it is unlikely that $100 per pair would be a good price unless there was a sudden run-up in shoes.

Now that I've laid out the basics of covered call writing and some of the factors affecting their price, I'll present some rules-of-thumb and strategic considerations:

1) When looking to write covered calls, one must pick a stock that is relatively volatile and therefore has relatively high option premiums. In general, unless you can get an annual return of about 20-30% from the premiums, option writing isn't worth doing. For example, if you could sell the 10 Apple 100 calls for $2500 every three months, or $10,000 per year, the return would be:

($10,000 for 1000 shares) / ($100,000 for 1000 shares)
$$= 10,000/\$100,000$$
$$= 10\% \text{ annual return.}$$

148

This return would not be enough for the risk being taken. If the 3-month calls were selling for at least $500 each, or $5000 every three months for 1000 shares, it would then be worth doing since the annualized return would then be 20% per year.

2) It is generally not worth writing covered calls unless one holds at least 500 shares (1000 is better). Unless you hold enough shares to get a decent premium, the broker will make more money than you will.

3) Write options further out-of-the-money if you want to keep the stock and think it will go higher. Write options more in-the-money if you think the stock is over-priced and really are just looking to sell the shares and get some downside protection. Obviously, the more in-the-money the shares are, the more likely you are to have the option exercised and your shares purchased at the strike price. If you think the stock has room to go higher, write the options at the next available out-of-the-money strike price or above. You'll get less premium, but are less likely to lose your shares and in any case will get more for the shares if they do end up being sold.

If you think the stock is overpriced and ready for a fall, writing in-the-money calls provides some level of downside protection and is really like selling the share at a little better price than they are currently trading (because the premium will normally be a little more than the difference between the current price and the strike price). Note that the IRS may consider the shares sold if the options you write are deep within-the-money, so check with your accountant if you are not sure.

The Risks of Covered Call Writing

Covered call writing is a conservative strategy, but it is still not risk free. It is probably more conservative than holding large blocks of shares outright, but not as conservative as holding mutual funds most of the time. Here are some of the special risks of covered call writing:

Risk 1: Capping possible gains
The main downside of writing covered calls is limiting capital gains. If a stock is at $43 per share and a call is written with a strike price of $45 per share, once the stock reaches $45 per share the maximum possible gain will have been realized. Even if the stock goes up to $100 per share after that, the investor would still only profit as if the stock had been sold at $45 per share.

The best way to guard against this risk is to only write covered calls on stocks that you believe are overpriced. You are essentially making a bet that the stock will not increase in price further when writing the call, so obviously it does not make sense to write calls on stocks that have a lot of room to run. If you are confident about the prospects of the stock in the near-term, just hold onto the stock and enjoy the gains. Also realize that in general when one sells a rising stock, one never ends up buying the shares back again. If you really believe in the long-term prospects, unless the stock is so over-priced that the potential for gains is extremely limited over the next several years, don't write covered calls.

Risk 2: Sale of the shares
The buyer of the call has the option to purchase the shares at the strike price at any time. Because it is to his advantage to hold the option as long as possible, it is unlikely that this will happen until the week of expiration or even the day of expiration, but it is still possible. If the shares are sold, capital gains will be due, brokerage fees will be charged for the sale of the shares, and one will need to pay brokerage fees again to buy the shares back if desired. The share price may have also increased before the shares are bought back. Never write a

covered call unless you can accept the sale of the shares at the strike price.

Risk 3: Increasing margin balances

Along with capping capital gains, the value of the call option will increase as the stock increases in price. Writing a call is like selling it short – thus gains in share price will cause the amount owed to replace the call to grow. Even though the loss for the investor is limited since the loss due to the increase in the value of the option will basically be directly offset by the increase in price of the stock, the amount "borrowed" from the brokerage firm will increase as the price of the call increases. If the value of the call increases beyond the amount of cash in the account, the brokerage firm will start to charge interest. If the position is held in a margin account, the brokerage firm may make a margin call and force the investor to sell stock, send in additional cash, or do some other action to cover the position.

The position can be closed by buying an offsetting call at any time (if you buy a call of the same expiration date and strike price, the two positions cancel each other). If one does so, however, and the stock then declines in price, a loss will be created.

In general the best protection is to have ample extra cash in the account to cover increases in the stock price. If the stock price increases above the strike price, close the position. Another position can be taken by writing another call at a higher strike price, although one runs the risk of suffering a string of losses this way and then seeing the stock price fall. It might be best to recover the loss simply by selling the shares.

Risk 4: Declines in the price of the stock

The effect of writing a covered call is to reduce the cost basis of the stock position (not for tax purposes, but in a total return sense). The act of writing the call therefore helps to offset losses due to the fall in the price of the underlying stock somewhat. For example, if a stock is at $45 per share and one collects a premium of $1.50 per share by writing a call, the stock could decline to $43.50 per share before the investor would start to lose money. Nevertheless, it is not uncommon for stocks to fall by 20-30% or more. When this happens, it is sometimes a difficult choice to either sit pat and wait for the stock to recover or write a call at a lower strike price and risking the stock rebounding in price and losing the shares at the lower price.

Perhaps the best defense against this risk is to buy stocks that have good long-term prospects and only write covered calls on stocks they seem overpriced in the near-term. If they then decline in price, you will have collected a bit of a gain to offset some of the price decline and still hold the shares for the long-term. Since you were planning to hold for the long-term anyway, the temporary decline in price should not concern you. The stock should recover and then some if given time. In addition, the gains realized from premiums from the calls can be used to buy more shares at the lower prices when the stock declines, so the investor can make an even bigger return when the stock recovers in price.

Risk 5: Taxes and Fees

Writing covered calls does result in trading more frequently, which will result in paying more brokerage commissions. In addition, the difference between the bid and the ask price, called the *spread*, is rather large for options. Since you will be selling at the bid price and buying offsetting options to close any positions at the ask price, this will reduce your total return. (The market-maker or the specialist will collect this difference between the bid and the ask each time you trade – it's good to be the market.) If trading in a taxable account, writing options will also result in short-term gains that will be taxed at normal income rates (this can change as new laws are passed, so check with an accountant).

Both of these factors will cause returns to be less than they could be. The best defense is to only write calls when the potential return is enough (premiums collected are at least 2% of the value of the shares) to compensate for these additional fees. Also, unless you absolutely need to, don't close positions by buying an offsetting call, Instead, allow the options to expire worthless whenever possible. Even though it may seem like a good idea to close the position and write a new one when the premium drops to almost nothing in the week before expiration, the fees paid will reduce gains. If the option is in-the-money near expiration, however, and it is likely that you will lose your shares, it may be worth closing the position rather than selling the shares and paying the brokerage fees to sell the whole position and then buy the shares back again.

To reduce taxes, trading in a tax advantaged account like an IRA should also be considered (although make sure there is plenty of cash since these accounts don't generally allow margin). And once again, only positions of at least 5 calls per trade (500 shares or more) should be considered for covered call writing to keep fees manageable.

Covered Call Writing – An Example
Having covered the mechanics of covered call writing and having gone into some of the risks, let's look at a practical example. This is to serve as an illustration of the technique and possible outcomes.

In 2012 I owned some shares of BJ's Restaurants, Incorporated. The company sells pizza and beer. They have a series of restaurants out west and sell gourmet pizza and microbrew beer. I think they have great prospects for the future since they are currently making gobs of money and have a lot of room to expand. These are key features for which to look when selecting stocks.

The market had realized their potential, however, and bid the shares up to really high values. The PE – price to earnings ratio - was over 50. Many fast growing companies have PE's in the 30's, but the 50's are a bit extreme. Typically PE will eventually return to a reasonable range, either because earnings increase, or because the price declines. Because of this, I expected the stock to either sit in the current range for a few years, waiting for earnings to catch up to the price, or the price to drop to a more reasonable level given current earnings. In any case, the stock was vulnerable to a sharp slide should the company miss earnings, a lawsuit occurs, or some other thing happens like another terrorist attack.

I didn't really want to sell the shares. I've found that when you sell a great stock, you end up putting the cash in something else and forgetting about the original company. Even if the price falls to reasonable levels or earnings increase, you may not have cash available at the time to take advantage of the lower prices. For this reason, I wrote a call option position on the shares. This would provide some income should the stock sit within a range for a long period of time, and reduce the loss somewhat should the shares fall in price.

When I was ready to write the calls, the shares were trading at about $46.50 per share, having completed a really fast run-up the week before. Looking at the option premium prices, I saw that the July options had reasonable premiums for the next out-of-the-money options, those with a strike price of $50. They were selling for about $1.60 per share. Writing May or June options did not provide enough in the way of premiums. The later options, like the Octobers, did not offer enough given the long time to expiration.

If I were more bearish, I might have sold the in-the-money options, the July $45s, and collect about $3.80 per share. If I did so, the price could have dropped to about $42 per share before I would lose some money. With the July 50's, if the price dropped below $45 I would lose money from the current value, but I would still make some money if the stock went up to $50. Even better, if the stock did not move very far up from the current position between then and July, I'd get to keep the entire premium from the options and maybe write another set of options. At $1.60 every three months, this is about $8.00 per year, or an effective "yield" of about 17%.

If the stock stayed at current prices or decreased, I'd just hold the options to expiration. After that I might continue to write calls as long as the stock was above $40 per share (I thought a price in the $30's the stock was more reasonable, yet still expensive, and in fact the price of the stock eventually fell to about $27 per share). If the stock moved above $50 per share and my shares got sold, I might have looked at writing covered puts at $45. In that transaction I would be obligated to buy the shares if they fell below $45 per share, but since I wanted the shares anyway it was a good way to make some money while possibly taking a new position in the stock. As long as I kept the cash in the account for that purchase, it was really like getting the shares below the current price. I could continue to write puts while the stock price was above $45 until I purchased the shares. I might even have dropped the strike price when writing future put options if the shares got near $45 per share and continued to lead the shares down until I finally bought them back in the $30's. The risk, however, was that the shares may have continue to climb and I would never have gotten to buy them back.

The shares could also have dropped well below $45, and then I would be stuck buying them at $45. Given that I was ready to buy them at a little below $45 anyway, it really was no more risky that putting in an order to buy the shares directly. Still, it wouldn't have been enjoyable to pay $45 for the shares when I could have them for $40 in the market.

In general, while covered call writing is tempting, I usually find that I do better just holding shares outright. If I think a stock has good prospects, limiting my potential gain by selling the gain above some strike price to someone else rarely makes sense. Likewise, if a stock is overpriced, it is often better to just sell it since the price swings can often easily outstrip any premiums collected from writing calls.

Nevertheless, I sometimes write covered calls anyway to remind myself of why I rarely write covered calls. It does have some entertainment value, is really good clean fun, and is a lot safer than Vegas. For retirement income in low interest rate, stagnant stock market environments, it also offers an alternative way to generate income.

Giving Money And Inheritance

If you have successfully accumulated wealth, there will likely be quite a bit remaining after you die. Just as you were conscientious with your money while you were growing wealth, you should be equally conscientious when leaving it to the next generation. Without appropriate planning, the inheritance could be a curse rather than a blessing.

Hopefully you have instilled the same fiscal values in your children as you have used yourself, and therefore they will be fairly well-off by the time you pass away and really not need your money. Your money could help them further along their way, but it might be more meaningful to do something for generations of your family beyond your children.
For example, you could create a trust that pays for the tuition

of your grandchildren and their descendants if they choose to attend college. Invested correctly and managed well, there is no reason that this trust could not last for many generations. This would be a much better legacy than simply passing the wealth down until it inevitably lands in the hands of a playboy who squanders it.

You might also consider giving a lot of your wealth to your children and grandchildren before you die. Rather than having them fight over your estate when you pass, you can start giving funds that you know you will not need as gifts each year. (These gifts might come with the stipulation that they will help you with expenses in your old age if needed.) While this may take time since gifts above certain limits are taxed during a year, given that you can make gifts to your children, their spouses, and even their children each year up to the IRS limit before gift taxes kick in, you can transfer quite a bit of wealth over a decade or more, all tax-free. Of course, careful planning with an accountant should be done, since Federal laws change from year-to-year, and each state may have its own rules.

Also, don't just think of your children. Perhaps there is a charity that you could help with some significant gifts. Maybe you could make a gift to a local school or arts center. Maybe you could just help out people who seem to need it, like the current "Tips for Jesus" phenomena happening in different parts of the country.

Other things to consider with inheritance planning:

1. Make sure you have a will and that it is valid. It is worth paying a couple of hundred dollars to do this right rather than using a $50 do-it-yourself will that may not stand up in court. Make sure that signed copies will be available to your personal representative,

maybe giving them a copy to hold.

2. Update your beneficiary information for your accounts as much as possible. These accounts can go straight to your heirs very easily.

3. Consider setting up a trust, and include assets such as your house and cars if you have a large net worth (about $1 million dollars or more). This can help avoid the hassle and expenses of probate. An issue your heirs may run into, however, is that few people understand trusts and most banks and other institutions are more used to doing things through probate. Appointing a tax lawyer as the trustee may be worth the cost to save some hassle.

4. Make sure everyone knows your plans ahead of time. If you are planning on cutting someone out of the inheritance, let them know while you are alive rather than leaving your heirs to fight things out after your death. Once again, consider giving some of your funds while you are still alive.

Chapter 9
The Rules For Serious Investing

The early chapters of this book provided some background on investing, including the various types of assets and their specific risks. The middle chapters of the book dealt with how investing should fit in with your life during each stage. Early on you were saving and investing what you could while getting your retirement accounts going. At mid-life you were continuing to invest and making smart choices to build wealth like buying used cars and limiting eating out. Finally you start to reach a stage in life where you have built up some wealth and can start to take advantage of it, doing things others can't and paying cash for it all. Finally, handling money in retirement and making your funds last was covered along with a discussion of inheritance planning.

Having dealt with the overall lifelong financial strategy, we now return to a discussion of the investing style introduced in Chapter 4. This style of investing, where assets are more concentrated than is traditionally recommended and company stocks are purchased for long periods of time, offers a good chance of beating the returns of the market. It is the financial management style described, where one frees up cash flow to allow for regular investing and minimizes the amount lost to things like interest and car value depreciation to allow one to pay for things like home repairs and college without needing to raid investment accounts, that enables the concentration and the long term investing.

As stated, I call this philosophy *Serious Investing*, in contrast to what many people do, which is more investing for entertainment than for making money. In the earlier chapter the basics of the philosophy were introduced. Here we expand upon the concept and provide the details needed to implement the strategy.

Serious investing is to trading what fishing with a net is to angling with a fly rod. It doesn't have all of the excitement that trying to jump in and out of stocks does, but in the end the serious investor will end up with a lot more money. Here I will first present the rules for serious investing and then go over each of them in detail. The rules for serious investing are:

1. Buy only the stocks you feel really strongly about.

2. Buy in sufficient quantities to make money when you are right.

3. Sell only based on the business, not based on what the market price is.

4. Reduce positions when they become too big to lose, but continue to ride winners.

5. Ignore the talking heads.

6. Don't get cute.

7. Learn from your mistakes (don't pay tuition to the market for the same lesson twice).

8. Constantly add to assets and limit liabilities.

9. Concentrate only on the long-term trends

1. Buy Only the Stocks You Feel Strongly About.

Because we aren't running a mutual fund with a billion dollars to invest, we can afford to be picky. We don't need to buy the stock we really like in a sector and it's three ugly step sisters just because we need to invest a gob of money. This is the advantage we, as small investors, have over the mutual fund managers, so use it. Only buy stocks you are very certain about.

Remember that we are buying stocks we plan to hold for a long, long time. Because the market and random events can move the market all over the place in the short-term, we aren't trying to catch some trend, or make a quick buck by trading in and out of a stock. It is difficult to time the market, or predict what will happen in the next year - that is a sucker's errand.

In serious investing, we are putting money into stocks we know will do well over the long-term. Because in the long-term what matters are the fundamentals of the company, this is much easier to predict than short-term fluctuations. For example, if a company has earnings that are growing by 15% per year, year-after-year, eventually it will produce a return of around 15% per year. It does this because all stocks trade within certain Price/Earnings ratios. If a stock's earnings grow by 15% for five years and the price does not move, the P/E will be cut in half (because the earnings will double while the price remains fixed). Investors will eventually see this imbalance and bid the price of the stock up until it once again goes within balance (or maybe even over-compensate and push it to a high P/E ratio). We can't say when the stock will move, we just know eventually it will.

We therefore look for stocks that we know will have earnings that will keep growing at a good clip over the long-term. We aren't interested in stocks that had great earnings this year because of a special situation – we want consistent growth. If we find this kind of stock, and it is trading at a reasonable price (P/E Ratio), we buy in. Otherwise, we build up cash and wait.

2. Buy in sufficient quantities to make money when you are right.

This second rule I only came to appreciate after reading J.D. Spooner's book, *Do You Want to Make Money, or Do you Just Want to Fool Around.* I have always been fairly good at picking stocks, but I would often pick a winner that would go up 10 or 20 dollars a share, only to make $1000 or so with my 100 share investment. Even in cases where the stock doubled or more, I would only make $2000-$3000 dollars. Had I bought 500-1000 shares, I would have made $10,000 to $30,000. This would have been enough to really make a difference.

So, if you are serious about making money in investing, be sure to buy enough shares of the companies that you select to make a serious profit when you are right. Note also that stocks don't tend to go to zero very often (although it does happen), but they do tend to double or triple. While you are also taking more risk when you buy more shares, your profits from the stocks that double when you are right will more than make up for the ones that go down 20-50% when you are wrong.

3. Sell only based on the business, not based on what the market price is.

As said numerous times in this book, you do want to cut any position that becomes so large that it would be a huge blow if something happened. I don't want to see any situations occur where an investor is out pricing his yacht one day because of gains in a stock and then seeing it all evaporate the next because it is discovered that someone has been cooking the books.   If a position becomes very large and takes over your portfolio, take some money off the table, pay the taxes, and shift some of the money into something else.

But by the same token, we are looking for long-term investment to take advantage of tax-deferred compounding and the reduction in trading fees and commissions that comes from trading infrequently.   We therefore don't want to sell stocks often.

Some strategies advise investors to sell out based on price movements.   There are strategies such as setting a stop loss at 10% below the purchase price so that if the stock drops by 10% you will cut your loss, or selling shares if the stock doubles in price or shows a pattern that indicates that the stock is topping and ready to turn down.   These strategies are not serious investing – this is listening to the market and not looking at the fundamentals of the company.   While holding onto a stock may require you go through a few downturns, it also avoids the possibility of missing a big movement up in the stock.   Because most stocks make their gains over very short periods of time, missing a big move up could significantly affect your return.

Note that often investors confuse price movements of a stock with the value or worthiness of a stock.   If a stock goes down in price by 10%, they think it is a "dog."   Likewise, if it goes up 10%, it is a winner.   Some individuals will therefore sell a stock if the price drops a bit, or rush in to buy because the stock went up.   Others may think it is a bargain since it fell in price and buy, or sell a stock they bought because it has gone up and now it is sure to go back down.

Spend a little time observing the market, and you'll discover, contrary to the writings of efficient markets theorists, that the short-term pricing given to stocks is at times irrational, and always unpredictable. It would be like walking into your favorite sandwich shop and discovering that one day sandwiches were $3.00 each, and the next day they were $1.00 each, even though there was no real difference in the sandwiches. Companies may post record earnings, beating all of the earnings estimates from analysts by several pennies a share, and yet the stock price may still fall 10% because earnings didn't beat the estimate by quite as much as people had expected. Likewise, a company may announce that business is terrible and therefore they are laying off 30% of their workers and the stock price may go up 10%.

The only reason to pay any attention to price at all is when deciding which stock to buy from a group of good candidates. If the price offered, relative to the "fair value" of the stock is a good deal, buy shares of that company. Likewise, if the price of a company has grown so fast that it will take years for the fair value to catch up with the current price, maybe sell some shares and put the money into a stock that is more reasonably priced. (Note that real estate speculators could have applied this rule near the end of the housing bubble where wages would take 20 years to catch up to some of the prices that were being asked for houses.)

It is therefore important to ignore the day-to-day fluctuations of the price of the stock and concentrate on the core business. Is the company making money and growing earnings each year? Is there business such that they have room for continued expansion? Do they have a good balance sheet (little or no debt and lots of assets) such that they could survive business downturns and outlive competitors?

For these reasons, I would advise only selling out of a stock if something about the fundamentals has changed. Maybe the new CEO has decided to turn your burger and ice cream chain into a large holding company, name it after himself, and have the company buy a variety of companies that have nothing to do with the restaurant industry. Maybe a company that has grown for years has just run out of room to expand and is going from a young growth company to a steady but slow-moving large cap. These are the reasons to sell a position. If you are selling based upon what the stock price is doing, you are just playing around and will miss out on the big gains.

So, in summary, look at the business when deciding which stocks to buy. Only worry about price in determining timing — when to buy — and even then don't concern yourself with price too much. Plan on holding the stock unless something changes on the business side of the stock. The only reason to sell a stock because of the price is if it has gone up in price so quickly that it would take years for the earnings to catch up.

4. *Reduce positions when they become too big to lose, but continue to ride winners.*

The main idea behind serious investing is attempting to beat the markets – and the mutual funds – by 1)buying stocks that have predictable long-term growth potential, 2)buying sufficient quantities of those stocks to make a good profit when they increase in price, and 3) holding for a long period of time so that market timing isn't an issue and fees and taxes are minimized. Because fewer stocks are bought than would typically be recommended for diversification, there will be greater fluctuations than would be seen with a basket of 100 stocks, say, but there is also greater potential for large gains because instead of buying the whole market, we are just buying the cream-of-the-crop.

This strategy is appropriate for someone who doesn't have a great deal of money to protect, and therefore it would be worse to have a low rate of return than it would be to suffer a loss in one or two positions. As the amount of money in the account grows, however, preservation of wealth becomes more important, and therefore more diversification will be needed.

The point of rule #4 is how to balance the two requirements. I propose that you stop looking at returns and percentages. Instead look at the amount of money really at risk. If you have a $5000 account to which you are adding a couple of thousand dollars per year from your earnings, you could probably stand to have a catastrophic loss, say of $3000 of the $5000. Percentage-wise this would be a 60% loss, but it is only $3000, in actuality. This is in return for the possibility of having a $5000 gain in a year. In a mutual fund, if you had a great year and made 20%, you would only have made $1000 for the year.

If you have been saving and making some good picks, and a position in the account grows to $30,000 in a $50,000 account, now it would be a huge setback if the stock had some bad news and fell 60%. This position should therefore be trimmed back and the money spread out to more stocks to limit the loss.

So, for each position, ask yourself if you would be willing to suffer the loss of the whole position. If the answer is yes, let it ride. If not, then trim the position back and diversify until you are comfortable.

5. Ignore the talking heads.

I remember one summer in college when I had just gotten cable and discovered CNBC. I was trading equity and index options and would spend part of the days when I didn't have classes watching the various shows. As each new analyst came on, I would listen and adjust my positions based on his or her reflections on the market. I watched the ticker for the OEX (S&P 100 Index) and the SPX (S&P 500 Index)

166

religiously. (There were no online quotes at that time, so you had to watch the ticker symbols going by. There also were no names written out, so you had to know the symbols by heart.) I would sit and think about the fluctuations in the value of my positions.

I had some good trades at first, but as time went on the markets turned against some of my positions. Eventually I gave up on some of the positions, letting the options expire and losing my whole bet. In the end I lost a great deal more than I even thought I was putting at risk because I kept adding to positions and averaging down, thinking that things were at a top or a bottom.

The moral of this story is that while watching the cable business news shows may have some entertainment value, the ideas, opinions, and recommendations of the various commentators and journalists are of no use to you. Even if they are right about a stock going up or falling to pieces, if they have a reasonably big audience, just their mentioning of the stock can send the price up or down several percentage points as soon as the words leave their lips.

If you try to trade based on their advice you will always be buying at a premium or selling at a loss. The same is true with analysts. If an analyst recommends a stock it will jump just because of the recommendation. If you wait a few days it will normally fall back to where it was because the crowd has moved onto something else.

Remember that the crowd follows the analysts and the commentators, and the crowd is notoriously famous for being exactly wrong. This is the reason for the old Wall Street axiom, "Buy on the rumor, sell on the news." When the news breaks, it is too late.

6. Don't get cute.

Sometimes instead of just doing something straightforward, we decide for some reason to do something elaborate.

For example, we have a position in a company that just didn't work out. We realize that the grand hopes we had for the company aren't going to materialize and we know it is time to cut our losses and put the capital to a better use.

Here the wise thing to do would be to just sell the stock. It doesn't matter that it once sold for more than it does now. The company no longer meets the criteria we use in selecting companies. Instead, we decide to get cute, and buy another 100 shares, wait the required 30 days to avoid a wash sale, and then sell the original shares to pocket the loss and offset some of our investment gains. We tell ourselves that then the stock will go back to where we bought it and we can avoid having a "losing trade."

Of course, the result is that the stock continues to fall and now instead of losing on just 100 shares, we have 200 shares going down in price. Serious investing is simple. Don't play around – you'll usually get burned and wish that you had just taken the simple path. If it is time to sell, sell. If you think a stock is a good buy, then buy it.

7. Learn from your mistakes. Or don't pay tuition to the market for the same lesson twice.

If you are investing in stocks (or anything else) you will sometimes make mistakes. Every investment will not result in a profit. Sometimes this will be of no fault of your own (things happen). Other times you will have done something foolish and it will usually be a costly mistake. I call this "paying tuition to the market." Another term might be "stupid tax."

Often one will not really learn something until there is a price tag attached. I've found that people (myself included) won't listen to the good advice that has been built up over a number of years in the investment community until they have lost money going against the advice. Some will be convinced that they somehow are different and will be able to time the short-term trends in the market. Others may not listen to the advice to just sell a stock when they have a big profit, decide to get cute and put in a limit order, and then watch as the stock falls and turns what should have been a good profit into a loss.

Everyone pays tuition to the market. Don't let losses affect you or make you swear off investing altogether. It is just part of your financial education. The important thing to take away from every loss (or missed gain) is a lesson on what you did wrong to make sure you don't make the same mistake in the future. Once you've paid for a lesson, don't pay for the same lesson again.

8. Constantly add to assets and limit liabilities.

This rule really has more to do with building wealth than investing. There is a finite amount of money that can be made through working. Unless one is a CEO and gets huge numbers of stock options (which actually is a form of investing), it is very difficult to grow wealthy simply from one's paycheck. Even if you live on half of your income, putting the rest away in a cookie jar, it will take your entire lifetime to save an appreciable amount. Even then, most of your wealth will have been destroyed by inflation. In order to grow wealthy, one needs to find a way to leverage his work such that each hour worked results in multiple hours worth of income.

An example of this is writing a book. The book can be sold several thousand times, so the effort that went into writing the book can be leveraged to create an "unlimited" stream of income. Another example is starting a business and hiring employees, where for each hour you work, you have several employees that are also working, and a part of their efforts results in income for you. Ownership in a business, however, will usually require a huge commitment of time, although some businesses may offer flexibility or not be all time consuming (usually if you are very lucky and there is someone running it that you trust).

If you are not gifted enough to write a good book (or don't feel like going through the effort to market it) and don't want to deal with the hassle of hiring employees, purchasing assets to gain leverage is the answer. Note, however, that there is typically some hassle involved with buying and holding assets as well. All assets require some degree of maintenance and/or protection. Stocks and bonds are usually kept in a brokerage account requiring yearly account fees, or at the minimum a safe deposit box. Assets such as real estate may require a great deal of upkeep, along with property taxes and other hassles.

Once assets are purchased, they start providing another source of income in addition to one's paycheck. While the amount of income will initially be very small, and some assets need to be kept for a long period of time before they start to produce income (or appreciate in value enough to be sold), as more and more assets are purchased one will derive an ever-increasing share of one's income from these assets and less and less from employment. The real growth comes when the assets are allowed to compound, such that income produced by assets is reinvested, purchasing more assets, which in turn creates more assets. Even Einstein marveled at the power of compound interest!

Unfortunately, few take advantage of the power of compound interest. In fact, they tend to let compound interest work against them. Virtually everyone will add liabilities until their entire paycheck is spoken for before the month starts. By buying things on credit, they end up paying for things many times over. Think about the dinner that is put on the credit card, held there for a year or so, and then rolled into a house mortgage. That dinner is then paid for over a period of 30 years and ends up costing 5 times as much as the original bill!

Liabilities are things that go down in value, don't provide income, and worst of all, often require money for maintenance. Probably the biggest liability most people have is cars, followed by their house (this is a smaller liability because it does pay for itself somewhat, but still limiting the size of one's house to what is really needed will aid in wealth creation). Some poor souls also have time shares, student loans, and the worst liability of all, credit card balances.

The secret is to reduce liabilities as much as possible so that each month you have control over a good share of your money. This will allow you to buy assets, which will provide an income, instead of paying huge amounts in interest. This requires waiting for things, but you will be far better off in the long run.

By constantly acquiring more assets while limiting liabilities as much as possible, anyone can become wealthy. It's that simple.

9. Concentrate only on the long-term trends.

This rule seemed particularly apt right after the bear market of 2008 and 2009. There was talk in the *Wall Street Journal*, *Barrons*, and other publications about a possible double dip recession. In Alan Abelson's lead column (Mr. Abelson was a delight to read but sometimes made you want to slit your wrists with his gloomy outlook) he talked about the possibility that we were not seeing a correction in a bull market, but a rally in a bear market. If he was right, that would have meant seeing lows below those seen in 2009. If that were the case, we really would have seen another "Great Depression" type market because there, too, there was a strong rally followed by more dismal behavior.

In 2008, like in the 1930's, there was also a lot of Government meddling in the economy and Keynesian theories put into practice. This very well may have been a factor causing the recession to drag out. (Note that there was a stock market crash in the '20s that no one every talks about because no action was taken and the markets recovered on their own within a year, as we saw after the 1987 crash).

So in 2012, I was thinking that maybe *Barrons* was right and we were in for a wild ride. But then again, maybe they were wrong, this is just a pull back and we'd see the bull market resume. There certainly was (and still is) a lot of fuel on the fire with interest rates as low as they were. It is always very difficult to know which way the market will go at times like that.

I did know, however, that the economy would eventually come back and the share prices of great companies would be higher than they were then. It is this long-term trend on which one needs to focus. All of the volatility we were seeing in 2008-2012 would be a little blip on the chart in 20 years.

It is in the times of the greatest declines that the opportunities for the greatest gains exist. Find the companies that have seen their earnings increasing and who are in good financial shape (no debt is a good sign) and snatch up their shares as they fall.

Don't expect to buy at the bottom, but just know that you're paying less today than you would have yesterday, and they'll be selling for more in the future. Focus on the long-term, and take advantage of the short-term fluctuations to set your positions.

Chapter 10
Investing in Mutual Funds

A lot of the material in this book deals with investing directly in common stocks and other types of assets rather than using mutual funds. This is how I invest most of my money and how I have done so for years. Investing this way cuts your costs since you won't be paying fees to a mutual fund manager (assuming you follow the strategies presented and therefore don't trade much). It also allows you the best chance you have of beating the market. By picking stocks, you are able to buy just your best stock picks, rather than buying everything in a mutual fund.

That said, there are certainly advantages to investing in mutual funds and many people only invest through funds. Additionally, even if you start holding individual stocks, once you have attained a substantial amount of money, more diversification is needed to help protect your assets against a loss. Mutual funds offer an easy way to diversify your holdings. You won't beat the markets, but if done properly, you won't lag the markets by very much either. Sometimes this is good enough. For this reason, this chapter is included to explain how to set up a portfolio using mutual funds as a complement to the serious investing philosophy.

With many employers giving employees 401k accounts rather than traditional pension plans, there is also a good chance you'll need to choose investments for a 401k account. Because very few 401k accounts offer anything but mutual funds, an understanding of mutual funds is needed even if you mainly choose individual stocks for your taxable portfolio. Note that having a 401k instead of a pension is often cited as a bad thing, but really the 401k is vastly better than traditional pension funds, as workers who actually contribute and leave the money in those accounts will find when they get ready to retire. The trouble is that too many people take the money out, while others invest too conservatively when they are young and too aggressively when they are older.

Mutual Fund Background
Mutual funds are agreements by which investors buy shares of the mutual fund rather than buying shares of stocks directly and then a professional money manager purchases shares of stock or other assets with the proceeds of the fund. Investors pay a fee to the manager and pay for investing expenses. The net profits and dividends are then distributed to the shareholders of the mutual fund depending on the number of shares they own. Typically mutual funds have an investment objective that guides how the money is invested, although the manager has some discretion.

The advantage of mutual funds is that they allow investors to easily achieve diversification without requiring the large sums of money that would be necessary to buy a large number of individual stocks directly. Investors with modest amounts to invest therefore often invest through mutual funds. Some large investors use mutual funds as well, either to reduce the hassle of picking stocks or because they believe in a large amount of diversification. Some novice investors may also feel that a professional money manager can do better at selecting stocks than they could do on their own (or they buy index funds, just hoping to match the market returns).

There is also a school of thought that believes that buying a large basket of stocks will be better than selecting a few stocks most of the time. Here, it is felt that the risk of selecting the wrong stocks is not adequately compensated for by the opportunity for additional gain. It is felt that the chances of doing better by picking individual stocks rather than by accepting the market return are low, and that the consequences of choosing the wrong stocks are too great, so it makes sense to buy mutual funds rather than trying to pick stocks.

The main disadvantage to investing in mutual funds is that the fund manager, because he has so much money under management, must buy not only his top picks but several other stocks in each sector. A second disadvantage is that there are costs associated with paying the manager and his staff, the cost of their research, and the administrative costs of managing the accounts. This means that the return of a mutual fund over time will almost always mirror the return of the market into which it is invested, minus the fees to the managers and expenses.

A third disadvantage is that an investor has little control over the investments made by the fund manager other than the selection of the type of fund. Care must be taken to verify that the investment objectives of the fund and the restrictions on how the fund may invest are consistent with the investor's investment objectives. A fund may have a name that implies it invests in small companies, but a look through the prospectus may reveal that it contains a lot of large companies as well.

Fund managers also sometimes play a sort of "game" to make their fund look more desirable. Because they must only report their holdings once a quarter, some managers buy shares in stocks that have done well during the quarter to make it look like they picked the winners. After reporting is done, they then sell those shares off and invest in their new picks. Not only is this practice deceptive, it also causes costs to increase since trading results in fees and taxes, further reducing the return.

The forth disadvantage of buying mutual funds is that the investor has no control over when capital gains are realized. This means that even if one is fully invested in a fund and does not sell shares, the investor will still receive capital gain distributions because the manager has sold shares at a gain and taxes must be paid on these gains. This reduces the ability of the investor to delay capital gain taxes and time the realization of gains.

Mutual funds come in different "flavors," with the most significant difference being between open-end and closed-end mutual funds. In an open-end mutual fund there is no fixed number of shares and investors buy and sell shares directly from the mutual fund company. The price is normally set based upon the value of the holdings owned by the fund, called the "net asset value," at the end of the trading day. If a person decided to buy 100 shares, for example, the fund would accept his investment and create 100 more shares of the mutual fund. The price of the shares would equal the value of the assets held by the fund, divided by the total number of shares, including the new shares being created. Note that because additional money is being provided by the new investor, the holdings of other investors in the fund do not change due to the new investment, but future returns may be affected until the mutual fund manager invests the new money.

Open-end mutual funds can only be purchased once a day and the price is determined by the value of the underlying stocks owned by the mutual fund. The disadvantage of this arrangement is that if a group of investors decide to sell shares of the mutual fund, the manager may be forced to sell investments to generate the money needed to pay the investors. This may force the manager to sell shares when prices are depressed (because people tend to leave funds when the price of stocks is declining), meaning he may need to sell stocks just when it would be a good time to buy. Funds also need to stay fully invested in order for the fund to perform well, so the receipt of new cash from investors may force the manager to buy shares when they don't feel prices are attractive. Some open-ended mutual funds restrict the number of times an investor may move funds in and out of the fund to prevent investors from trying to time the market since this drives up costs.

With a closed-end mutual fund the number of shares is fixed (although some funds issue more shares at times) and the shares are then traded on a stock exchange between investors just like a stock. This means that purchases or sales of shares of the fund have no effect on the amount of money in the fund. Exchange Traded Funds, or ETF's are a relatively new form of closed-end mutual fund designed to mimic specific sectors of the market. The advantage of closed-end funds is that fund managers don't need to sell shares of stock when shares of the mutual fund are sold. They can therefore time their stock purchases and sales without worrying about the activities of holders of the fund, and trading costs can be kept lower.

Some open-end mutual funds have had issues in the past in that investors were allowed to buy shares at the closing price of the previous day after the opening of the next day. These investors were then able to sell the shares quickly and realize a profit at the expense of the long-term holders of the fund. This practice is normally illegal, but it happens every so often nonetheless.

Closed-end mutual funds are not affected by sales and there is no way to game the system because the shares are traded among investors. The price of the mutual fund shares is set based on what investors are willing to pay for them at any given time. This means that the price may be greater or less than the value of the holdings per share. If the price is greater, the mutual fund is said to be trading at a *premium*. If less, then it is said to be trading at a *discount*.

Investors may sell the shares at a discount, particularly if the mutual fund has performed so badly that they decide that they are willing to give up a bit of the underlying value just to put their money somewhere else with a better return. Likewise, investors may pay a premium for a mutual fund if they believe the returns will be better than those of their competitors over time or the mutual fund pays a dividend that is large compared to other income investments. Some people do not like closed-ended funds because the price of the fund may not reflect the changes in the value of the underlying assets because of this premium or discount. For example, the asset value of a fund may increase by 20% in a year but the fund price may only increase by 15% because investors think the market may soon turn downwards.

A special risk of closed end funds is that they sometimes convert into open-end funds. When this occurs, the fund's price per share quickly changes to its net asset value. If the shares were bought at a premium to asset value, a quick loss will occur.

Factors when selecting funds
Selecting mutual funds is far less involved than selecting individual stocks. Because mutual funds invest in a wide variety of stocks (or bonds, or other asset classes), virtually any mutual fund will provide about the return of the market, minus fees and trading expenses. The main things to consider when selecting a mutual fund are therefore expenses and investment objectives.

Investment fees when shares are purchased or redeemed are called the "load." Many funds are "no load," meaning they don't charge a fee for purchases or sales, but they still have operating fees and expenses, which are important considerations. In general, because most mutual funds will track the market over long periods of time minus fees and expenses, minimizing fees and expenses will maximize returns.

In selecting mutual funds, many people would buy the one that performed the best over the last year or two. After all, that manager might have some secrets that allow him to generate those 20% returns. Why would someone want to settle for a paltry 5% return when one could get 20%? However, one must be careful to read that little disclaimer that is at the bottom of all mutual fund advertisements: "Past performance may not be indicative of future results." Just because a stock fund or a sector of the market does well a certain year does not mean that it will continue to outperform its peers.

In fact, because the fund has done well it is more likely that the stocks in the fund will be overpriced and that it will lag its peers the next year. Likewise, just because a stock fund does poorly in any given year does not mean that it will do poorly the next year. It is the result of this chasing performance that most people buy funds right before they are ready to decline and sell them just before they are ready to shoot up.

Rather than using past performance in selecting mutual funds, one should consider the following:

1) Check the fees compared to other similar funds. If fees are high (greater than 1%), it would be wise to change to a less expensive fund in the same sector. Index funds tend to have very low fees because there is no need to pay a team of professional managers to research investments as is done in regular mutual funds.

2) Evaluate the asset type in which the fund invests. If you are in an emerging markets fund, the performance will likely be all over the map with some spectacular years and some dismal years. If you buy a bond fund it will not perform as well as a stock fund over a long period of time, but in years when the market declines or stagnates it will do better than a stock fund.

For example, in 2008 stocks fell more than 20% while bond funds generally had a positive return. It is therefore a good idea to own funds in different segments of the market with the balance depending on how long you have before needing the money.

Deciding Between Mutual Funds and Stocks

Deciding which way is appropriate for you to invest in stocks – through individual stocks or through mutual funds – depends on several factors, including your time available to research investments, your tolerance for volatility, your investment objectives, and your interest and ability to pick stocks.

Buying individual stocks means selecting, from the thousands of choices available, the small basket of stocks you would like to own. It also means deciding when to buy, and probably more importantly, when to sell. Buying individual stocks means being able to control your emotions and determining the best choices for a position while prices are moving up 100% or down 50% in a single year, or even a period of a few weeks. It also requires more study to learn the mechanics of putting in trades, the nuances of things like ex-dividend dates, and more bookkeeping when it comes to income taxes.

By buying stocks directly one can outperform the market. As stated in the Chapter 9 in the discussion on serious investing, instead of buying all ten of the stocks in a market sector like a mutual fund manager, you can pick just the top one. If you have a talent for sorting out the good businesses from the bad, you can do much better than the market return. You also have the advantage that you don't need all of your picks to be good, just one or two to be great.

There are certainly advantages to mutual funds as well, however. In buying a mutual fund, you are pooling your money with that of thousands of other investors. That pool of money is then used to buy 100, 200, 500, or even 1000 different stocks. Buying mutual funds gives automatic diversification, which will reduce the chance of losses and generally reduce the amount of volatility so that the value of your portfolio will be more stable. While there are years when the market (and therefore mutual funds) will move up or down 40%, most years will result in swings of 20% or less. Also, while buying mutual funds guarantees only matching the market at best, minus fees and expenses, mutual funds are easily bought, and once purchased require almost no maintenance at all.

Given the choice between individual stocks or mutual funds, one should buy mutual funds if most of the following are true:

1. You tend to be worried by large fluctuations in your portfolio value. If a drop of 20% would cause you to sell and hide under a rock, individual stocks aren't for you. If you would take advantage of the lower prices to buy more shares, you have the right psychology.

2. You don't have the desire to learn about the markets or do the research needed to find good stocks. Many people have other things that they would rather be doing than reading the *Wall Street Journal* and *Money Magazine*. If this is true of you, maybe mutual funds would be a better choice.

3. You don't have time to do the research to find good stocks. Because mutual funds are the market, finding good mutual funds requires a lot less time than finding good stocks. Granted, once you have found a basket of good stocks the time required to maintain the portfolio drops dramatically, so long as you are investing for the long-term, but it does take an initial investment of time.

4. You have a lot of money. The more money you have, the more important it is to have the proper diversification to reduce the chances of a large loss. As said, a person who has $2000 to invest can well afford the loss of the $2000 in a single stock, provided he is raising money from his salary and investing regularly. A person with $1 million cannot afford a loss of the whole $1 million from large positions in a few stocks. A good portion of that money, say 50%, should be in mutual funds. Another portion, say 30%, should be in several large, solid, dividend paying stocks and bonds. The remainder can be in larger positions in individual growth stocks, if desired. As one's wealth grows, a portion should be diverted into mutual funds. That portion should then grow with the value of the portfolio.

5. You can't leave things alone. People who are constantly trading will never make money in individual stocks. If you find yourself constantly watching CNBC, unable to stick to a position for long periods of time, you would be better off buying mutual funds and using some of the proceeds each year to fund a trip to Vegas. At least that way you'll get a change of scenery and drinks will be included.

Setting up a 401K

As stated in the start of this chapter, a common use of mutual funds is in a 401k account. With more and more companies going from defined benefit, or pension plans, to defined contribution, or 401K plans, individuals are finding themselves needing to determine how to save and grow their money for retirement themselves.

While it may seem daunting to some, being able to manage and control your money has benefits. You don't run the risk of being thrown into the government pension pool should your company go bankrupt or not contribute enough to the pension plan. Likewise you can choose where the money is invested. Also, often you will find that the rate of return you receive will be greater when invested in stocks than that from a traditional pension plan where the benefits are defined. (Remember that the pension plan is invested in the stock market too, so they can't promise to pay as much as the market might provide in return.) Finally, when you are ready to retire, you will have all of the money available at once, rather than getting a monthly or yearly check from the pension plan.

With the 401k, because this is your retirement savings, you can't afford to take the kind of risks that you can take with your regular investment account. Also, most 401k accounts are limited in the investment choices, and some funds restrict trading, so they really aren't suited for stock picking and rapid growth anyway. It is best to just set things up and then touch it rarely.

With a 401k, the goal is to grow funds while minimizing risk to reasonable levels while still earning enough to outpace inflation. Because a savings account will always pay slightly less than the rate of inflation, the only options for a 401k account are stocks and bonds (and real estate assets through an REIT fund if available as one of the options).

While substantial diversification is not desirable for our regular investment account (at least in the beginning) if we want to beat the market, because we really aren't able to pick stocks in a 401k account–being limited normally to mutual funds–diversification is desirable so that we can at least get market returns. While it is tempting to try to time the market, shifting from small to large stocks when we think large stocks will outperform small, or shifting out of stocks and into bonds when we feel that the market is near a peak, experience has shown that the rapid rises in stocks tend to occur over very short periods of time. If we try to time the market and are wrong, we'll end up doing far worse than the market.

The good news is that this makes 401k investing very simple, requiring very little time. A good 401k plan will have a selection of funds that will include a money market, large growth stocks, small growth stocks, bonds, value stocks, and international stocks. Some funds may also include options such as emerging markets, REIT's, commodities, junk bonds, and convertibles. Here's the strategy when you're 10 years or more away from retirement:

Invest equal amounts in the lowest cost funds in each of the main categories: large growth stocks, large value stocks, small growth stocks, small value stocks, and international stocks (20% in each). If you don't mind some volatility, you can also put a lessor percentage in the other, more volatile funds (aggressive growth, emerging markets, etc...), but these positions should be smaller, for example, 5% in each of these with 15% in the main categories).

Each year (pick a date such as your birthday), rebalance the account so that the percentage invested in each fund are the same as you started with. This will mean that if the value funds do better than the growth funds during the year, for example, you will be selling some of the value funds and buying some of the growth funds – selling high and buying low.

As discussed in Chapters 7 and 8 for an IRA, when you start to get within about 10 years of retirement, start shifting some of the funds over to bonds and income producing stocks, which are less volatile (but also tend to produce lower returns), and then into cash (the money market fund) as you get very close to retirement for the money that you will need within the next five years. Note that if you do have a taxable investment account, you should raise cash there first, as previously described. You want to allow your retirement accounts to grow tax deferred as long as you can.

Looking at your investments as a whole, at retirement you will therefore have about 40% of the funds in bonds and income producing stocks, 5% in cash, and 55% in growth and value stocks. As you get older you'll continue to shift funds into cash as needed to cover five years' worth of expenses and more funds into bonds and high yielding stocks since you can no longer stand the kind of market fluctuations that you could while you still had another source of income and didn't need the funds right away.

So easy, right? Just spread out the money, leave it alone, rebalance once in a while, then start to take some out as you eye retirement. Unfortunately, most people are terrible managers of their 401k accounts. Here are the most common mistakes people make:

1. Not Investing Enough. In order to have enough saved for a comfortable retirement, you must put away enough from each paycheck. A good rule of thumb is to put away 10-15% of your take-home pay. Note that this is your contribution, without counting the contribution of your employer. As stated in the chapter on investing early in your career, a good strategy is to put enough away to receive the full company match, then fund a standard or Roth IRA, then put anything additional left over into your 401K up to the maximum. If you still have more money left (lucky you) just invest in a standard taxable account. Note that investing early means a lot more than investing later, so start off investing as much as you can right when you start your first job.

2. Keeping Too Much in Cash. Some individuals are scared of investing in stocks and therefore leave the money in a money market. Remember that money market funds will pay a few percentage points less than inflation, so each year you are actually losing money. While stocks can move up and down, over long periods of time (which is what you have when saving for retirement) they will outpace inflation by several percentage points. The difference between a 401K filled with stocks and one filled with money market funds will be millions of dollars. So, take the plunge and invest. If you are nervous, just don't look at the balance more often than every five years or so – things will be fine on autopilot.

3. Trying to Time the Market. It can be scary to listen to the commentators at times. They will often talk about a slowing of the economy or overheated markets. The trouble is, most big market moves occur in very short periods of time. If you pull your money out and miss a big move upwards, your return will be far less than it would have been if you had left things alone. While it can be tempting, trying to time the market and pull funds out just in time is a bad idea. Just let things be. If it makes you feel better, increase your contribution amount during market dips.

4. Concentrating in One Area. Like trying to time the market, some individuals think that certain areas of the market will do better than others. Just remember that everyone else has the news that you have. If a market segment is hot, the prices will have already risen to account for it. It is best to just spread your money out over several different types of stocks and market segments.

5. Keeping Too Much in Bonds. The percentage you hold in bonds should be no more than your age. For example, a 20 year-old should have no more than 20% of her savings in bonds (with the rest in stocks). While it may seem safer to have a larger bond portfolio, once again you'll be cheating yourself of a lot of return if your bond mix is too high. A little bit of cash also makes up for a deficiency in your bond mix (a 60-year old with 10 years' worth of expenses in of cash and the rest in stocks is just as safe as one with 60% bonds).

6. Taking Money Out Early. This is probably the worst thing one can do – withdraw funds before retirement age. Some see their 401K as found money, taking out funds to pay off credit cards, buy a house, or just spend the money. Not only do you pay a huge penalty for doing this, each dollar you remove in your 20's will result in the loss of about $128 in retirement. That $10,000 you took out to pay off credit cards just cost you $1.28 million! Live within your means and let your 401k grow. Unless you will be thrown out on the street if you don't, there is no reason to remove funds from a 401k.

Likewise, taking a loan against your 401k is also a bad idea. If you end up leaving the company (on purpose or involuntarily), that loan will become due at once. If you lack the money to repay the loan immediately, you will be penalized just as if you took an early withdrawal. If you need to borrow money, see a bank, not your 401K.

Chapter 11
An Analogy for Building Wealth

Stocks and bonds can be tools to help you build wealth. They can also just be ways to earn more money to spend. They are a way to make your wealth grow faster, but until you make the transition in thought from being a worker who lives from paycheck to paycheck to being an investor who creates income sources that replenish themselves, you will never become wealthy. Put another way, to paraphrase financial author and teacher Dave Ramsey, "You can't out-earn stupid."

The fact is, most people have only a few dollars left over at the end of the month after they factor in all of their obligations. It doesn't matter if they make $30,000 per year or $300,000. Left alone, obligations will build up to swallow all free cash in one's budget. The insurance bills. The gym memberships. The clothes and the haircuts. The cable TV bill. The mortgage payment and the payment on the condo. Growing wealthy involves investing, and that can't be done with $30 per month. So instead of just concentrating on making things balance on a budget, begin to look at your wealth "pool."

Picture a large, crystal-clean pool of water that you can go to as needed, dip in your cup, and get a cool drink. At first you fill your wealth pool by hauling containers of water and dumping them into it. Most people spend their whole lives hauling containers until they are too tired and weak to haul anymore. In the end hopefully they have enough in their wealth pool to last them the rest of their lives.

Obligations are like leaks from your pool. The interest you pay puts a drain on your wealth pool, causing water you've worked hard to carry to run out onto the ground and away without you getting any use out of it. If you are able to haul water quickly –

you have a large income and work a lot – you may be able to keep your pool fairly deep even with some holes. Still, if you have enough leaks in the walls of your pool, you will eventually be doing all you can just to keep the level up. Many high earners have so many leaks in their pool that water is constantly gushing out. They end up a paycheck away from serious financial issues even though they make as much in a year that others earn in ten.

Assets are like water lines attached to a large lake that you add to your pool. They are sources of water that you don't need to haul. At first these lines tend to be small and you barely notice the difference, but with time, as you add more water lines and use the income from earlier lines to build later ones, it becomes less and less important to haul water in with containers.

So in addition to looking at your income and spending, take a look at your water lines and leaks from your pool. At the top of your budget make a list of your water lines, your estimated return for the year from each line, and the amount of income from those lines you will use and the amount you will reinvest. Sum the total income from all of your water lines.

At the bottom, list your leaks – the obligated expenses you have. Your mortgage, your car payment, your student loan payment, any memberships you have, timeshare fees, etc.… Your leaks include anything you have that you pay each month, such that the money is obligated before you even earn it.

Subtract the total of your leaks from the total of your water lines. If this number is positive, you'll be gaining water in your pool even if you do nothing. If the number is negative, your pool will always be draining and you'll have to work even harder to keep it filled.

See which leaks you can plug. Can you focus and pay off a loan so that you no longer have the payment anymore? Are there things you buy on subscription or automated draft that you could buy periodically when you felt like it instead? Remove as many subscriptions as practical, keeping only those that you know you would buy every month anyway.

Concentrate on plugging leaks. As you plug each leak, dedicate the money you would have spent on the leak some months to investments so you can build more water lines. Don't look at this as losing the money – you can always sell the investment and spend the money later if you want. Instead you are storing it and using it to generate more income. Avoid taking on new obligations, instead paying cash for things as you go. With time see if you can get the inflow from your water lines to exceed your obligations. At that point your pool will be filling without you doing anything.

Once your asset inflows exceed the outflows from your obligations, your wealth will really start to grow. You can start siphoning off some of the excess to improve your life. Maybe if you have $10,000 net income each year from assets you can take $3000 each year and take a week-long vacation. Maybe you can add something to your home or your yard each year. Because you are spending from your asset income instead of your working income, the pool will replenish itself.

By looking at what drains from your wealth pool and adding water lines, you can get a better picture of your financial situation and make the changes that will make growing wealth easier. It all starts and ends, however, with consistency. Spend less than you make. Put money away and invest regularly. Build your asset portfolio and fill your pool.